SOUTH-WESTERN
MATHMATTERS **3**
An Integrated Approach

ANSWER KEY
STUDENT SUPPLEMENT/
ACHIEVEMENT TESTS

CHICHA LYNCH
Capuchino High School
San Bruno, California

EUGENE OLMSTEAD
Elmira Free Academy
Elmira, New York

SOUTH-WESTERN PUBLISHING CO.

Cover Photo Photographer: Wayne Sorce © June 1988
Audio Kinetic Sculptures by George Rhoads

RETEACHING 1–1

1. T   2. F   3. T   4. F   5. T   6. T
7. F   8. T
9. $\{x\}, \{y\}, \{x, y\}, \varnothing$
10. $\{7, 9, 11, 13 \ldots\}$
11. $\{-4, -6, -8, -10 \ldots\}$
12. 2   13. 6   14. –15   15. 24

RETEACHING 1–2

1. F   2. T   3. F   4. F   5. T   6. F

7. $-1\frac{3}{8}, \frac{1}{5}, \sqrt{2}, 3.9,$ as marked

8.

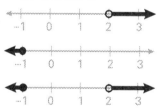

9. 0.8   10. –0.8   11. 0.8   12. –0.8   13. 0.8
14. –0.8

RETEACHING 1–3

1. 7, 10   2. 2   3. 2, 3, 5, 7, 10
4. Roster notation: {–1, and all real numbers less than –1 or greater than 2}
   Set-builder notation: $\{x | x$ is a real number and $x > 2$ or $x \leq 1\}$

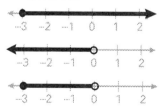

5. Roster notation: {–3, and all real numbers between –3 and 0}
   Set-builder notation: $\{x | x$ is a real number and $-3 \leq x < 0\}$

RETEACHING 1–4

1. 0.39   2. –4.9   3. 4.3   4. $-\frac{2}{7}$ 5. $-1\frac{3}{5}$

6. $-1\frac{8}{10}$ or $-1\frac{4}{5}$ 7. –3.7   8. 1.1   9. –1.1
10. 3.7

RETEACHING 1–5

1. –12.96   2. –27   3. 0.5   4. 6.3   5. $1\frac{3}{7}$

6. $-\frac{1}{2}$ 7. $-1\frac{5}{6}$ 8. $-9\frac{3}{8}$ 9. 0.552

10. –5   11. 0.025   12. 0.2   13. 0.02   14. 5
15. 20

RETEACHING 1–6

1. $288.60   2. 2:02 p.m.   3. 98   4. $4.11
5. $3.10

RETEACHING 1–7

1. 7.28   2. $-\frac{3}{4}$ 3. 7   4. –12.6   5. –0.001
6. –0.225   7. 2.56   8. –3   9. x^{12} 10. a^6
11. b 12. $a^4 b^6$ 13. 1   14. x^3 15. $7^8 a^4$
16. x^7

RETEACHING 1–8

1. x^{-8} 2. $-x^4$ 3. x^0 or 1   4. b^{15} 5. m^{-4}
6. c^{-10} 7. a^{-11} 8. r^3 9. 4.2093×10^4
10. 7.29×10^8 11. 7.4×10^{-3} 12. 6.21×10^{-4}
13. 7,300   14. 0.00652   15. 42,100
16. 0.00091

RETEACHING 1–9

Methods will vary for Exercises 1–6.
1. $40.12   2. 90   3. $418.00   4. $7,400
5. Yes, because 10 – 4 = 6 and 5 · 1.12 < 6
6. $194.37

RETEACHING 2–1

Rules may vary for Exercises 1–8; sample answers given.
1. –12, –15, –18 (–3)
2. 35, 42, 49 (+ 7)
3. 0.01, 0.001, 0.0001 (÷10)
4. 64, 128, 256 (× 2)

5. $\frac{16}{3}, -\frac{32}{3}, \frac{64}{3}$ (×(–2))

6. $-\frac{1}{16}, \frac{1}{64}, -\frac{1}{256}$ (×(–$\frac{1}{4}$))

7. $\frac{1}{6}, \frac{1}{7}, \frac{1}{8}$

8. 125, 216, 343

9. 12, 18, 24, 30, 36, 42

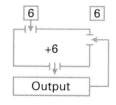

10. 5; –25; 125; –625; 3,125; –15,625

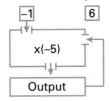

RETEACHING 2–2

1. Function: Yes
   Domain: {–1, 0, 1}
   Range: {–4, –2, 2}
2. Function: No
   Domain: {6}
   Range: {–2, –1, 0, 1}
3. Function: Yes
   Domain: {0, 1, 5}
   Range: {1, 2, 4}
4. Function: Yes
   Domain: {1, 2, 6}
   Range: {1, 2, 6}
5. Function: No
   Domain: {4, 7}
   Range: {4, 7}
6. 3   7. –13   8. 5   9. –197   10. 2   11. 22
12. 0   13. –10

RETEACHING 2–3

1.

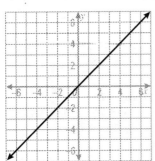

2.

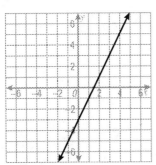

3. 6   4. 8   5. 1   6. 16   7. 10   8. 1
9. 14   10. 10

RETEACHING 2–4

1. 44   2. –4   3. –14   4. 8   5. –45
6. –72   7. $1\frac{1}{2}$ 8. 98   9. 20
10. $46 - n = -21$; $n = 67$
11. $n \div 11 = 0.5$; $n = 5.5$
12. $2n = 6^2$; $n = 18$

RETEACHING 2–5

1. 5   2. 2   3. 3   4. –6   5. 20   6. 4
7. 1   8. –10   9. 3   10. –5   11. 12   12. 4
13. 11   14. 6   15. 20   16. 6

RETEACHING 2–6

1. $x = 1$

2. $x = -1$

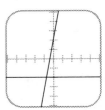

3. $x = 2$ 4. $x = 1$ 5. $x = -3$ 6. $x = -2$
7. $x = 0$ 8. $x = 3$ 9. $x = -5$ 10. $x = 4$
11. $x = -1$ 12. $x = 1$ 13. $x = -4$ 14. $x = 5$
15. $x = -10$ 16. $x = -3$ 17. $x = -2$

RETEACHING 2–7

1. $x \le 3$

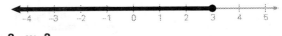

2. $x > 2$

3.

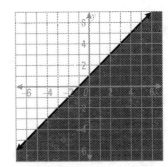

4.

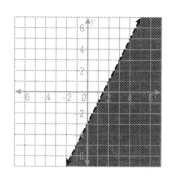

RETEACHING 2–8

1.

	A	B	C	D
1	20	100	30	70
2	40	200	60	140
3	60	300	90	210

2.

	A	B	C	D
1	Corp	Ind	Govt	Total
2	5,000	A2*0.6	A2*0.2	A2 + B2 + C2
3	A2 + 5,000	A3*0.6	A3*0.2	A3 + B3 + C3

	A	B	C	D
1	Corp	Ind	Govt	Total
2	5,000	3,000	1,000	9,000
3	10,000	6,000	2,000	18,000

RETEACHING 2–9

1. Mean: 102
Median: 103
Mode: 103

No.	Tally	Freq
100	III	3
101		0
102		0
103	IIII	4
104	I	1

2. Mean: 213
Median: 213
Mode: 215

No.	Tally	Freq
210	I	1
211	I	1
212	II	2
213		0
214	I	1
215	III	3

RETEACHING 2–10

1. a.

1	7 6 7 9
2	8 1 9 3
3	6 2 4
4	5 2 4
5	
6	5

b. Outlier: 65
Cluster: 16 – 45
Gaps: 45 – 65

c.

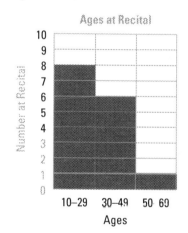

2. a.

10	1
11	
12	5 6 8 9 5
13	1 0 1 2
14	2 6 3 1
15	
16	3

b. Outlier: 101 and 163
Cluster: 125 – 146
Gaps: 101 – 125, 146 – 163

c.

Cost of In-line Skates

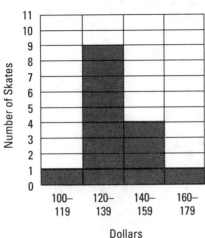

RETEACHING 3–1

1. *S, Q, R*
2. $\overleftrightarrow{TQ}$, $\overleftrightarrow{QR}$, $\overleftrightarrow{RT}$
3. $\overrightarrow{QR}$
4. 5   5. 4   6. 8   7. 12   8. 54   9. 45

RETEACHING 3–2

1. 60°   2. 140°   3. 80°   4. 100°   5. 20°
6. 40°   7. 60°   8. 40°   9. 90°   10. 50°
11. 40°   12. 70°

RETEACHING 3–3

1. point *Q*, 3
2. $\overline{LN}$ 3. $\overline{OQ}$, $\overline{NR}$, $\overline{MS}$
4. 42°   5. 138°   6. 138°   7. 69°

RETEACHING 3–4

Check students' drawings for Exercises 1–8.
8. Perform segment bisector construction. Then bisect one of the angles with vertex at midpoint. Repeat.

RETEACHING 3–5

1. 71°   2. 52°   3. 38°   4. 90°   5. 180°
6. 29°   7. 29°   8. 29°   9. 151°   10. 119°
11. 61°   12. 151°

RETEACHING 3–6

1. The fifteenth figure will consist of a regular pentagon with sides of 14 units; having 13 pentagons with sides decreasing in size by 1 unit in its interior. All pentagons sharing a common endpoint.

2. The fifteenth figure will consist of 16 rays with a common endpoint.

3. 8, 12, 16, 20   4. 72 right angles

RETEACHING 3–7

Sample answers given for Exercises 1–4.
1. Converse: If points *A, B, C,* and *D* are collinear, then points *A, B, C,* and *D* lie on both plane *L* and plane *M*. Original statement is true. Converse is false. Counterexample: $\overleftrightarrow{AD}$ lies on plane *L*; and plane *L* is parallel to plane *M*.
2. Converse: If ∠*IQJ* and ∠*HQJ* are obtuse angles, then *m*∠*IQJ* + *m*∠*HQJ* > 180°. Original statement is false. Counterexample: *m*∠*IQJ* = 30° (acute angle) and *m*∠*HQJ* = 170° (obtuse angle); the sum of their measures is 200°, which > 180°. Converse is true.
3. Converse: If three lines are coplanar, they have one point in common. Original statement is false. Counterexample: 2 coplanar lines intersecting, with third line intersecting that plane at only that one point. Converse is false. Counterexample: 3 parallel lines.
4. Converse: If two lines are not coplanar, then they are skew. Original statement and converse are true.

RETEACHING 3–8

1. 1. given
   2. supplementary angles
   3. vertical angles
   5. multiplication
   6. right angle
   7. perpendicular lines

2. **Statements**
  1. $g \perp h$
  2. $\angle 3$ is a right angle
  3. $m\angle 3 = 90°$
  4. $m\angle 3 = m\angle 1 + m\angle 2$
  5. $m\angle 1 + m\angle 2 = 90°$
  6. $\angle 1$ and $\angle 2$ are complimentary angles
Reasons
  1. given
  2. definition of perpendicular lines
  3. definition of right angle
  4. vertical angles theorem
  5. substitution
  6. definition of complimentary angles

RETEACHING 3–9

1. 5: Maria; 8: Keisha; 13: Leah; 36: Jo
2. 500 Elm: Grocery; 538 Elm: Boutique; 524 Elm: Cafe; 544 Elm: Studio

RETEACHING 4–1

1. $x = 60$ 2. $x = 7$ 3. $x = 120$ 4. 90° 5. 22°
6. 68° 7. 158°

RETEACHING 4–2

1. 1. given
  2. $\angle B \cong \angle E$; $\angle A \cong \angle D$
  3. $\overline{BE} \cong \overline{BE}$
  4. addition property of equality
  5. $\overline{AB} + \overline{BE} = \overline{AE}$; $\overline{DE} + \overline{BE} = \overline{BD}$
  6. substitution property
  7. ASA postulate
2. **Statements**
  1. $\overline{MN} \parallel \overline{OP}$, $\overline{MN} \cong \overline{OP}$
  2. $\angle NMO \cong \angle MOP$
  3. $\overline{MO} \cong \overline{MO}$
  4. $\triangle OMP \cong \triangle MON$
  Reasons
  1. given
  2. If two parallel lines are cut by a transversal, alternate interior angles are equal.
  3. reflexive property
  4. SAS postulate

RETEACHING 4–3

1. $\overline{AB} \cong \overline{BC}$, $\overline{BE} \cong \overline{BD}$
2. definition of vertical angles
3. vertical angles theorem
4. $\triangle ABE \cong \triangle CBD$
5. CPCTC 6. 3 cm 7. 35° 8. 9 m

RETEACHING 4–4

1.    2.

3.   4.

5. true 6. true 7. true 8. false 9. true
10. true

RETEACHING 4–5

1. midpoint 2. $\overline{MZ}$ 3. right 4. 90°
5. 90° 6. transitive property
7. reflexive property 8. SAS 9. $\overline{YZ}$
10. contradicts 11. false 12. true

RETEACHING 4–6

1. < 8 mm and > 2 mm
2. < 5.8 in. and > 3.4 in.
3. < $10\frac{1}{2}$ cm and > $5\frac{1}{2}$
4. $\angle I$, $\angle H$, $\angle G$ 5. $\overline{MO}$, $\overline{MN}$, $\overline{NO}$
6. Longest: $\overline{PR}$ 7. Longest: $\overline{UT}$
  Shortest: $\overline{QR}$ Shortest: $\overline{ST}$

RETEACHING 4–7

1. 139° 2. 135°; 45° 3. 117° 4. 75°; 150°
5. 144° 6. 60° 7. 3600°

RETEACHING 4–8

1. $a = 14$ 2. $a = 4$
  $b = 19$ $b = 3$
  $c = 54$ $c = 2.5$
  $d = 54$ $d = 2.5$
3. $a = 6$
  $b = 90$
  $c = 45$
  $d = 6$
4. 96° 5. 90° 6. 42° 7. 48°

RETEACHING 4–9

1. 17   2. 7   3. 14   4. 8
5. $\angle L = 31°$; $\angle J = \angle I = 149°$
6. $\angle M = \angle N = 78°$; $\angle P = \angle O = 102°$
7. $\angle Q = \angle T = 72°$; $\angle R = \angle S = 108°$
8. $\angle V = \angle W = 54°$; $\angle U = \angle X = 126°$

RETEACHING 4–10

1.

Second iteration   Third iteration

2.

Second iteration   Third iteration

3. *Answers will vary. Check students' drawings.*

RETEACHING 5–1

1. 11   2. 288   3. 80   4. 36   5. 128   6. 20
7. 3400   8. 1.085   9. 435   10. 8000
11. 3200   12. 0.023
13. $\frac{48}{54}$, or $\frac{8}{9}$
14. $\frac{12}{15}$, or $\frac{4}{5}$
15. $\frac{8}{16}$, or $\frac{1}{2}$
16. $\frac{5}{2000}$, or $\frac{1}{400}$
17. $\frac{520}{4000}$, or $\frac{13}{100}$
18. $\frac{3000}{5500}$, or $\frac{6}{11}$

RETEACHING 5–2

1. $P = 20$ m
   $A = 20$ m^2
2. $P = 43.6$ ft
   $A = 116.85$ ft^2
3. $P = 30$ m
   $A = 30$ m^2
4. $C = 25.12$ in.
   $A = 50.24$ in.^{2}
5. $P = 49.4$ cm
   $A = 140.4$ cm^2
6. $P = 22$ in.
   $A = 24$ in.^{2}
7. $P = 66$ yd
   $A = 209$ yd^2
8. $C = 37.68$ mm
   $A = 113.04$ mm^2

RETEACHING 5–3

1. $P = \frac{1}{9}$, or 0.1111
2. $P = \frac{9}{60} = \frac{3}{20}$, or 0.15
3. $P = \frac{3}{15} = \frac{1}{5}$, or 0.2

4. $P = \frac{24}{36} = \frac{2}{3}$, or 0.6667
5. $P = \frac{4308}{58560} = \frac{1077}{14690}$, or 0.0736
6. $P = \frac{154}{420} = \frac{11}{30}$, or 0.3667

RETEACHING 5–4

1. 340 yd^2; $5,100
2. 250 yd^2; $3,750
3. 557 yd^2; $8,355
4. 180 yd^2; $2,700
5. 93.6 yd^2; $1,404
6. 32 yd^2; $480

RETEACHING 5–5

Sample answers are given for Exercises 1–6.
1. Triangular prism
   Points A, B, C, D, E, F
   ABC, DEF
   $ABED$ and DEF; $\overline{DE}$
2. Rectangular pyramid
   Points A, B, C, D, E
   $BCDE$
   ADE and $BCDE$; $\overline{DE}$
3. Hexagonal prism
   Points $A, B, C, D, E, F, G, H, I, J, K, L$
   $ABCDEF, GHIJKL$
   $DEKJ$ and $ABCDEF$; $\overline{DE}$
4. Rectangular prism
   Points A, B, C, D, E, F, G, H
   $ABCD, EFGH$
   $EFGH$ and $ADFE$; $\overline{EF}$
5. Pentagonal pyramid
   Points A, B, C, D, E, F
   $BCDEF$
   $BCDEF$ and ABC; $\overline{BC}$
6. Triangular pyramid
   Points A, B, C, D
   BCD
   BCD and ABC; $\overline{BC}$

RETEACHING 5–6

1. 800 in.^{2} 2. 151.89 yd^2 3. 82.14 ft^2
4. 96 cm^2 5. 556 mm^2 6. 240 m^2

RETEACHING 5–7

1. 205.38 cm^3 2. 0.484 m^3 3. 3.768 in.^{3}
4. 2411.52 cm^3; 2009.6 cm^3
5. 1500 in.^{3}; 1230 in.^{3}
6. 74.088 m^3; 66.15 m^3
7. 276 ft^3 – 120 ft^3 = 156 ft^3

RETEACHING 5–8

1. 25.78 mm; ±0.005 mm
2. 18.15 mm; ±0.005 mm
3. $1\frac{3}{4}$ in.; $\pm\frac{1}{8}$ in.   4. 0.0005 mm
5. ±0.05 cm   6. ±0.005 mm   7. $\pm\frac{1}{16}$ in.
8. $\pm\frac{1}{32}$ in.   9. $\pm\frac{1}{64}$ in.
10. Upper: 185.91 mm; Lower: 185.61 mm

RETEACHING 6–1

1. –1   2. 0   3. 2   4. –3   5. $\frac{1}{2}$ 6. $\frac{3}{2}$
7. undefined   8. $\frac{4}{3}$ 9. 1
10.

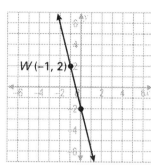

11.

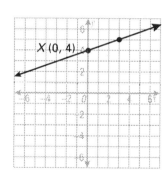

RETEACHING 6–2

1. $m = -2$
   $b = 0$
2. $m = -3$
   $b = 10$
3. $m =$ undef.
   $b =$ none
4. $m = 1$
   $b = 6$
5. $m = -2$
   $b = 6$
6. $m = 3$
   $b = 1$
7. $m = -1$
   $b = 3$
8. $m = \frac{1}{4}$
   $b = \frac{1}{2}$
9. $m = 0$
   $b = 8$
10. $m = -2$
    $b = \frac{5}{2}$
11. $y = -2x + 3$
12. $y = x - 4$
13. $y = 5x$
14. $y = 3x + \frac{5}{6}$
15. $y = -7$
16. $y = -4x - 1$

RETEACHING 6–3

1. Parallel: 1
   Perpendicular: –1
2. Parallel: $-\frac{9}{8}$
   Perpendicular: $\frac{8}{9}$
3. Parallel: $-\frac{3}{4}$
   Perpendicular: $\frac{4}{3}$
4. Parallel: $\frac{1}{7}$
   Perpendicular: –7
5. parallel
6. neither
7. parallel

RETEACHING 6–4

1. $y = \frac{2}{3}x + \frac{1}{3}$
2. $y = -2x - 4$
3. $y = 5$
4. $y = -3x - 7$
5. $y = \frac{1}{2}x + \frac{1}{2}$
6. $y = \frac{1}{3}x - 4$
7. $y = -x$
8. $y = x - 2$
9. $y = 5x + 3$
10. $y = \frac{1}{2}x - 1$
11. $y = 2x$
12. $y = \frac{1}{5}x - 2$
13. $y = 11x + 18$
14. $y = 5x - 31$

RETEACHING 6–5

1. The solution is (–2, 1).

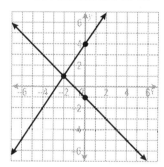

2. The solution is (4, 2).

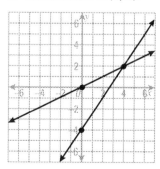

3. The solution is all points on the line.

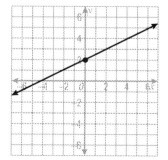

4. The solution is (–4, 0).

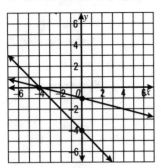

5. The solution is (4, –2).

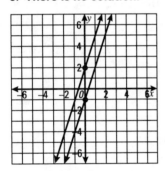

6. There is no solution.

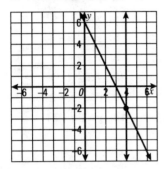

RETEACHING 6–6

1. $C = 2x + 150$ 2. $I = 5x$
3.

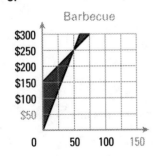

4. 50 tickets   5. $250   6. Loss

RETEACHING 6–7

1. (3, 1)   2. (1, –5)   3. $(-\frac{1}{3}, \frac{10}{3})$ 4. (20, –30)
5. (28, 3)   6. (–8, –35)   7. (3, –1)   8. (–4, 12)
9. 8 in. by 6 in.

RETEACHING 6–8

1. (3, 2)   2. (2, 2)   3. (–9, –1)   4. (4, 4)
5. Infinite number of solutions, dependent system
6. (2, 6)   7. (–3, –5)   8. (2, 0)   9. 4 in. by 8 in.

RETEACHING 6–9

1. 35
2. $6,750 @ 9%, $3,250 @ 7%
3. 23 quarters, 19 dimes
4. 61
5. 94
6. 20 L of 80% solution, 10 L of 50% solution

RETEACHING 6–10

1. a. $\begin{bmatrix} -3 & 4 \\ 1 & -2 \end{bmatrix}\begin{bmatrix} x \\ y \end{bmatrix} = \begin{bmatrix} 12 \\ 6 \end{bmatrix}$
   b. 2
   c. (–24, –15)

2. a. $\begin{bmatrix} 5 & 1 \\ 1 & -1 \end{bmatrix}\begin{bmatrix} x \\ y \end{bmatrix} = \begin{bmatrix} 10 \\ 5 \end{bmatrix}$
   b. –6
   c. $(2\frac{1}{2}, -2\frac{1}{2})$

3. a. $\begin{bmatrix} 1 & -1 \\ 1 & 1 \end{bmatrix}\begin{bmatrix} x \\ y \end{bmatrix} = \begin{bmatrix} 16 \\ 10 \end{bmatrix}$
   b. 2
   c. (13, –3)

4. a. $\begin{bmatrix} 2 & -2 \\ -1 & 3 \end{bmatrix}\begin{bmatrix} x \\ y \end{bmatrix} = \begin{bmatrix} 8 \\ 12 \end{bmatrix}$
   b. 4
   c. (12, 8)

RETEACHING 6–11

1. $y \geq -\frac{1}{2}x + 2$
   $y < \frac{1}{2}x$

2. $y > -2$
   $y \geq -4x - 4$

3.

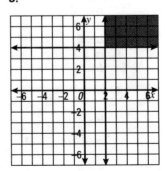

4.

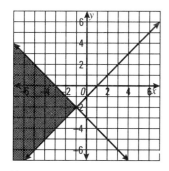

5.

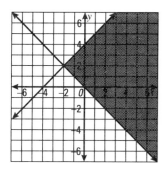

RETEACHING 6–12

1. 20 at (5, 0)

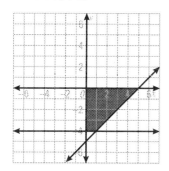

2. −6 at (0, 2)

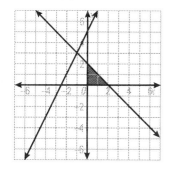

3. 0 at (0, 0)

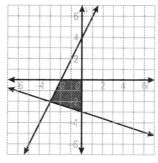

4. −2 at (0, −2)

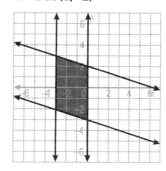

RETEACHING 7–1

1. $a = 6$ 2. $b = 35$ 3. $c = 63$ 4. $d = 8$
5. $e = 27$ 6. $f = 11$ 7. 75 tiles
8. $4,500 and $7,500

RETEACHING 7–2

Explanations may vary for Exercises 1–4; sample given.
1. No, $\angle B = 143°$ and $\angle F = 127°$, so corresponding angles are not congruent.
2. Yes, all corresponding $\angle$s are congruent and all corresponding sides are in proportion.
3. Yes, all corresponding $\angle$s are congruent and all corresponding sides are in proportion.
4. No, $\angle J = 143°$ and $\angle N = 127°$, so corresponding angles are not congruent.
5. 140
6. 15

RETEACHING 7–3

1. 15 m   2. 12 in.   3. 0.25 km   4. 6 mi
5. $\frac{2}{5}$ in.   6. 13.5 cm   7. $\frac{3}{4}$ in.   8. 33 cm

RETEACHING 7–4

Estimates may vary for Exercises 1–5; samples given.

1. $\frac{2}{10} = \frac{x}{180}$
   About 36 gal

2. $\frac{50}{70} = \frac{90}{x}$
   About $126

3. $\frac{60}{200} = \frac{x}{800}$
   About 240 rejections

4. $\frac{10}{3} = \frac{12,000}{x}$
   About $3,600

5. $\frac{30}{1} = \frac{x}{3}$
   $x \approx 90$
   $90 \times 20 = 1,800$
   About $1,800

RETEACHING 7–5

Reasons may vary in Exercises 1–5; sample given.
1. Yes, AA   2. Yes, SAS   3. No   4. Yes, SSS
5. Yes, AA   6. No

RETEACHING 7–6

1. 15   2. 8   3. 40.0   4. 15   5. 4   6. 1.8

RETEACHING 7–7

1. 12   2. 17.5   3. 6   4. 28   5. 1   6. 175
7. 7.5   8. 3

RETEACHING 7–8

1. 62.5 ft   2. 18 ft   3. 70 cm   4. 24 m
5. 22 m

RETEACHING 8–1

1. $D'(0, 4)$; $E'(3, 5)$; $F'(2, 1)$
2. $D'(-7, 4)$; $E'(-4, 5)$; $F'(-5, 1)$
3. $A'(6, -4)$; $B'(2, -2)$; $C'(3, -6)$
4. $A'(-6, 4)$; $B'(-2, 2)$; $C'(-3, 6)$
5 and 6.

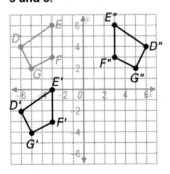

RETEACHING 8–2

1. $A'(3, 4)$; $B'(4, -3)$; $C'(2, -1)$
2. $A'(-2, -1)$; $B'(-4, -2)$; $C'(-1, -3)$
3. $A'(2, 1)$; $B'(2, 3)$; $C'(-1, 4)$

4.

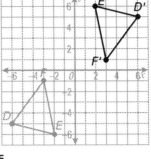

5.

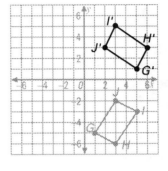

RETEACHING 8–3

1. $P(5, 5)$ 2. $P(6, 2)$ 3. $P(-3, -2)$
4. $P(6, -6)$ 5. $M(3, 2)$ 6. $M(-2, 1)$ 7. $M(4, 3)$
8. $M(-4, -4)$ 9. $P(4, 2)$

RETEACHING 8–4

1. $(-6, 4)$
2. $(2, 1)$
3.

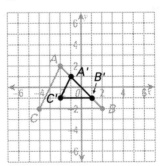

4.

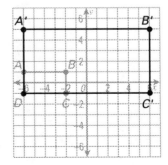

5.

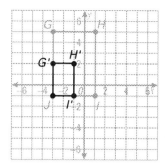

4.

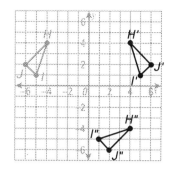

RETEACHING 8–5

1.

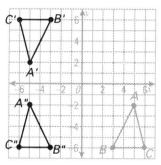

5.

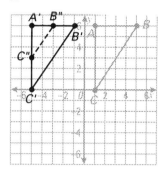

2.

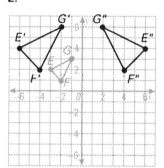

6.

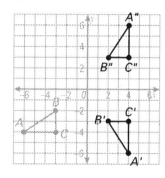

3.

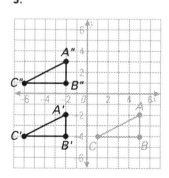

RETEACHING 8–6

1. 1   **2.** 2   **3.** 7   **4.** 8

5. $\begin{bmatrix} 12 & -14 & 8 \\ 3 & 14 & 0 \end{bmatrix}$

6. $\begin{bmatrix} 10 & -6 & 7 \\ 13 & 13 & 1 \end{bmatrix}$

7. $\begin{bmatrix} 11 & 5 & -7 \\ 5 & 13 & 9 \end{bmatrix}$

8. $\begin{bmatrix} 13 & -3 & -6 \\ -5 & 14 & 8 \end{bmatrix}$

9. $\begin{bmatrix} 30 & -90 & 80 \\ 60 & 50 & -10 \end{bmatrix}$

10. $\begin{bmatrix} 28 & 12 & -4 \\ 28 & 32 & 8 \end{bmatrix}$

11. $\begin{bmatrix} 20 & 10 & -30 \\ -10 & 25 & 35 \end{bmatrix}$

12. $\begin{bmatrix} 180 & -100 & 0 \\ -60 & 180 & 20 \end{bmatrix}$

13. $\begin{bmatrix} 11 & -5 & -4 \\ 2 & 15 & 13 \end{bmatrix}$

14. $\begin{bmatrix} 97 & -47 & -1 \\ -23 & 98 & 12 \end{bmatrix}$

15. $\begin{bmatrix} 16 & -24 & 23 \\ 25 & 23 & -1 \end{bmatrix}$

16. $\begin{bmatrix} 41 & -9 & -2 \\ 5 & 43 & 7 \end{bmatrix}$

RETEACHING 8–7

1. $\begin{bmatrix} -32 & -9 \\ -41 & 18 \end{bmatrix}$

2. NP

3. $\begin{bmatrix} -15 & 45 & -40 \\ 45 & 72 & -33 \end{bmatrix}$

4. $\begin{bmatrix} 15 & -68 & 57 \\ 33 & -53 & 54 \end{bmatrix}$

5. $\begin{bmatrix} 30 & 9 & -49 \\ 24 & 24 & -28 \end{bmatrix}$

6. $\begin{bmatrix} -20 & -10 & 30 \\ -30 & 39 & 81 \end{bmatrix}$

7. $\begin{bmatrix} -35 & 5 \\ 42 & 21 \end{bmatrix}$

8. NP   9. NP   10. NP

RETEACHING 8–8

1. $\begin{bmatrix} -3 & 3 & -2 \\ 2 & 1 & -3 \end{bmatrix}$

2. $\begin{bmatrix} -3 & 2 & 6 & -3 \\ 3 & 5 & 2 & -2 \end{bmatrix}$

3. $\begin{bmatrix} 1 & 4 & 3 \\ 1 & 3 & 4 \end{bmatrix}$

4. $\begin{bmatrix} -1 & -4 & -3 \\ -1 & -3 & -4 \end{bmatrix}$

5. $\begin{bmatrix} -1 & -3 & -4 \\ 1 & 4 & 3 \end{bmatrix}$

6. $\begin{bmatrix} 1 & 3 & 4 \\ -1 & -4 & -3 \end{bmatrix}$

RETEACHING 8–9

1. $39   2. $59   3. $46   4. $98   5. $105
6. $144   7. $74   8. $21   9. $49

RETEACHING 9–1

1. $\frac{3}{10}$, 0.3, 30%

2. $\frac{2}{10}$ or $\frac{1}{5}$, 0.2, 20%

3. $\frac{3}{10}$ or 0.3, 30%

4. $\frac{1}{8}$, 0.125, 12.5%

5. $\frac{3}{8}$, 0.375, 37.5%

6. $\frac{3}{8}$, 0.375, 37.5%

7. 10 times   8. 20 times   9. 30 times
10. 50 times   11. 30 times   12. 0 times
13. 20 times   14. 30 times

RETEACHING 9–2

Answers will vary for Exercises 1–3; check students' simulations.

RETEACHING 9–3

1. $\frac{2}{11}$

2. $\frac{4}{11}$

3. $\frac{5}{11}$

4. $\frac{2}{6}$ or $\frac{1}{3}$

5. $\frac{4}{6}$ or $\frac{2}{3}$

6. $\frac{3}{6}$ or $\frac{1}{2}$

7. $\frac{3}{6}$ or $\frac{1}{2}$

8. $\frac{5}{36}$

9. $\frac{31}{36}$

10. $\frac{11}{36}$

11. $\frac{25}{36}$

12. $\frac{2}{8}$ or $\frac{1}{4}$

13. $\frac{6}{8}$ or $\frac{3}{4}$

RETEACHING 9–4

1. $\frac{1}{36}$

2. $\frac{1}{12}$

3. $\frac{1}{4}$

4. a. $\frac{3}{50}$

   b. $\frac{1}{4}$

   c. $\frac{3}{20}$

   d. $\frac{3}{100}$

5. a. $\frac{3}{18}$ or $\frac{1}{6}$

   b. $\frac{1}{9}$

   c. 0

   d. $\frac{1}{72}$

RETEACHING 9–5

1. Permutation, 120 ways
2. Combination, 84 ways
3. Combination, 10 ways
4. Permutation, 336 ways
5. Combination, 10 ways

RETEACHING 9–6

1. 10 cups
2. 40 cups
3. a. 86   b. No   c. 50%
   d. *Answers will vary. Sample given.*
      The greatest test score is 98; the least is 47. Half of the data is in the box clustered around the median, 86.
4. a. 25%   b. 75%   c. 50%

RETEACHING 9–7

Answers will vary for Exercises 1–2; sample answers are given.
1. It appears Lou's grade point average for the second quarter is three times his first quarter average when actually the increase was small. Change the intervals on the vertical scale so they are consistent. Possibly compare the average to other quarters in other years.
2. The graph to support the position that the school will be overcrowded will have small increments on the scale representing number of students. A line graph supporting this position would have a steeper line, making the number of students appear to increase dramatically.

RETEACHING 9–8

1. 2; $\sqrt{2}$ or 1.4   2. 10; $\sqrt{10}$ or 3.2
3. 5.2; $\sqrt{5.2}$ or 2.3   4. 8; $\sqrt{8}$ or 2.8
5. 11.6; $\sqrt{11.6}$ or 3.4   6. 69.2; $\sqrt{69.2}$ or 8.3
7. 31.6; $\sqrt{31.6}$ or 5.6   8. 121.2; $\sqrt{121.2}$ or 11.0
9. 5; $\sqrt{5}$ or 2.2   10. 1; $\sqrt{1}$ or 1
11. Exercise 10   12. Exercise 8   13. Second

RETEACHING 10–1

1. $6\sqrt{2}$ 2. $10\sqrt{3}$ 3. $11\sqrt{2}$ 4. $2\sqrt{14}$
5. $4\sqrt{30}$ 6. $4\sqrt{6}$ 7. $4\sqrt{23}$ 8. $16\sqrt{3}$
9. $60\sqrt{5}$ 10. $24\sqrt{14}$ 11. 200 12. $168\sqrt{3}$
13. 140 14. $\frac{2\sqrt{3}}{3}$ 15. $2\sqrt{5}$ 16. $\frac{\sqrt{15}}{5}$
17. $\frac{2\sqrt{6}}{3}$

RETEACHING 10–2

1. 5.0 cm   2. 26.0 mm   3. 5.3 cm
4. 13.4 yd   5. 5.7 in.   6. 5.0 ft   7. no
8. yes   9. no   10. yes   11. yes

RETEACHING 10–3

1. $IK = 10\sqrt{3}$ cm   2. $MN = 9\sqrt{3}$ cm
   $IJ = 20$ cm $LN = 18\sqrt{3}$ cm
3. $OQ = 2$ in.   4. $RT = 6$ ft
   $QP = 2\sqrt{2}$ in. $ST = 6\sqrt{3}$ ft
5. $VW = 5\sqrt{2}$ in.   6. $YZ = 3$ in.
   $XZ = 2\sqrt{3}$ in.
7. $BC = 5\sqrt{3}$ m   8. $FD = 12\sqrt{3}$ m
   $AB = 10\sqrt{3}$ m $FE = 12$ m
9. $GI = 10\sqrt{2}$ yd
10. 1. $IK = 17.3$ cm
    2. $MN = 15.6$ cm; $LN = 31.2$ cm
    3. $QP = 2.8$ in.
    4. $TS = 10.4$ ft
    5. $VW = 7.1$ in.
    6. $XY = 1.7$ in.; $XZ = 3.5$ in.
    7. $BC = 8.7$ in.; $AB = 17.3$ in.
    8. $FD = 20.8$ m
    9. $GI = 14.1$ yd

RETEACHING 10–4

1. 83°   2. 54°   3. 75°   4. 52°   5. 124°
6. 42°   7. 92°   8. 15°   9. 184°

RETEACHING 10–5

1. | Pub | 52% | 187° |
   |-----|-----|------|
   | Broad | 24% | 86° |
   | Cable | 18% | 65° |
   | Movie | 6% | 22° |

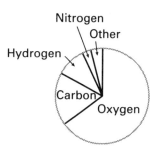

Media Market Value

2. | O_2 | 65% | 234° |
   |-------|-----|------|
   | H_2O | 10% | 36° |
   | N | 3% | 11° |
   | C | 18% | 65° |
   | Oth. | 4% | 14° |

Elements in 150-lb Person

RETEACHING 10–6

1. 30   2. 5   3. 6   4. 9   5. 8   6. 40
7. 12   8. $12\frac{2}{3}$

RETEACHING 10–7

Check students' constructions for Exercises 1–4;
final figure is shown.

1.   2.

3.

4.

10. $56m^2n^3 - 49mn^3 - 42n^3$

11. $-24a^4b^2 + 16a^3b - 8a^3b^2$

12. $-36x^3y^2 + 48x^3y^3 - 24x^2y^3$

13. $56x^3 - 42x^2 + 126x$

14. $-200m^3 + 150m^2 - 100m$

15. $8a^3b^2c^3 - 8a^3b^4c^2 - 8a^2bc^2$

RETEACHING 10–8

Check students' constructions for Exercises 1–4; final figures shown.

1.

2. Dime

3.

4. *Answers may vary. Sample given.*
   1) Draw a circle. Then construct a polygon using a compass and straightedge. 2) Draw a triangle. Then circumscribe a circle about it.

RETEACHING 11–1

1. $4b^2 - 3b + 4$
2. $6a - 2b$
3. $9m^2 - 2mn - 8$
4. $2c^2 + 3cd + d - 7$
5. $8a^2 - 7a + 15$
6. $4b^2 - 2bc - 11c^2$
7. $11t^2 - 8t + 7$
8. $11x^2 - 6xy - 3y^2 - 12$
9. $10j^2 - 12j + 12$
10. $-6m^2 - mn - n^2 + 18$
11. $5k^3 - 6k^2 - 5k + 2$
12. $5ab^2 - 6ab + 6a^2b - 8$

RETEACHING 11–2

1. a^2bc
2. $72xy^3z$
3. $32m^3n^2$
4. $3b^2 - 24b$
5. $3m^3 - 6m^2n$
6. $ax^2 - bx^2$
7. $-9d^2 - 54d$
8. $-6a^3b^3 + 14a^2b^2$
9. $4x^3 + 12x^2 - 24x$

RETEACHING 11–3

1. $1, 4ab^2; 2, 2ab^2; 4, ab^2; a, 4b^2; 2a, 2b^2; 4a, b^2; b, 4ab; 2b, 2ab; 4b, ab$

2. $1, 9c^2d^2; 3, 3c^2d^2; 9, c^2d^2; c, 9cd^2; 3c, 3cd^2; 9c, cd^2; c^2, 9d^2; 3c^2, 3d^2; 9c^2, d^2; d, 9c^2d; 3d, 3c^2d; 9d, c^2d; cd, 9cd; 3cd, 3cd; 9cd, cd$

3. $1, 14c^2d^3; 2, 7c^2d^3; 7, 2c^2d^3; 14, c^2d^3; c, 14cd^3; 2c, 7cd^3; 7c, 2cd^3; 14c, cd^3; c^2, 14d^3; 2c^2, 7d^3; 7c^2, 2d^3; 14c^2, d^3; d, 14c^2d^2; 2d, 7c^2d^2; 7d, 2c^2d^2; 14d, c^2d^2; d^2, 14c^2d; 2d^2, 7c^2d; 7d^2, 2c^2d; 14d^2, c^2d; cd, 14cd^2; 2cd, 7cd^2; 7cd, 2cd^2; 14cd, cd^2$

4. $1, 10xy^3; 2, 5xy^3; 5, 2xy^3; 10, xy^3; x, 10y^3; 2x, 5y^3; 5x, 2y^3; 10x, y^3; y, 10xy^2; 2y, 5xy^2; 5y, 2xy^2; 10y, xy^2; y^2, 10xy; 2y^2, 5xy; 5y^2, 2xy; 10y^2, xy$

5. $4\ mn$

RETEACHING 11–4

1. $3(3x + 4)$
2. $a(a + 4)$
3. $7a^2(a - 2)$
4. $3y^2(5y^2 - 4z)$
5. $x^3(8x^2 - 5x + 2)$
6. $4mn(4m^4 + 1 - 2n)$
7. $9y^3(3y^2 - 1)$
8. $4b^2(3a^2 + 2a + 4)$
9. $y^2(9y^2 - 3y + 1)$
10. $2x^4(4x^6 - 12x + 3)$
11. $3y^2z(-3 - 4y^2z^2 + 5yz^3)$
12. $a^3b(b - 3a)$
13. $3x(4x^3 + 2x - 1)$
14. $5(3k^3 + k + 2)$
15. $3j(-6j^2 + 4j - 3)$
16. $3c(12cd^2 - 3d + 4)$
17. $x^3y^4(xyz^3 - y^2z^4 - x^3)$
18. $2f(f^2 - 9f + 4)$

RETEACHING 11–5

1. $x^2 - 11x + 24$
2. $a^2 + 5a + 6$
3. $m^2 - 14m + 45$
4. $w^2 + 11w + 18$
5. $n^2 - n - 56$
6. $p^2 + 3p - 54$
7. $2t^2 + 2t - 12$
8. $10s^2 - 36s + 32$
9. $6b^2 + 29b + 28$
10. $8 + 2x - x^2$
11. $a^2 + 2ab + b^2$
12. $12m^2 + 18mn - 12n^2$
13. $9a^2 - 4b^2$
14. $15c^2 - 4cd - 32d^2$
15. $120x^2 - 44xy - 28y^2$
16. $4x^2 + 4xy + y^2$
17. $4x^2 - 4xy + y^2$
18. $4x^2 - y^2$

RETEACHING 11–6

1. $(2a + 3b)(5c - 2d)$
2. $(a + 2b)(c - d)$
3. $(e - f)(g + 3h)$
4. $2(3w + 2x)(2y - z)$
5. $4(2p - q)(3r - 5s)$
6. $(3a + 2b)(c - d)$
7. $(4w - x)(9y - 2z)$
8. $3(a + 3b)(3c + d)$
9. $2(4q - r)(s + 2t)$
10. $(2a + 3b)(x + y + z)$
11. $(2a - b)(3x + 2y + 4z)$
12. $2(m + 2n)(9r - 2s - 3t)$

RETEACHING 11–7

1. $(r - 8)^2$
2. $(t + 9)(t - 9)$
3. $(w + 6)^2$
4. $(c + 8)^2$
5. $(a + 4)(a - 4)$
6. $(x + 4)^2$
7. $(3y + 7)(3y - 7)$
8. No factors
9. $4(b - 5)^2$
10. $(3z + 2)^2$
11. $(5a - 6)^2$
12. $4(x + 4)(x - 4)$

RETEACHING 11–8

1. $(a + 3)(a + 2)$
2. $(x - 10)(x + 1)$
3. $(m + 8)(m - 2)$
4. $(t - 7)(t + 5)$
5. $(s + 8)(s + 3)$
6. $(k + 5)(k - 4)$
7. $(r - 9)(r + 8)$
8. $(x - 7)(x - 4)$
9. $(y + 6)(y + 2)$
10. $(b - 6)(b - 4)$
11. $(d + 4)(d + 5)$
12. $(p - 7)(p + 3)$
13. $(k + 12)(k - 10)$
14. $(r - 10)(r + 9)$
15. $(z + 15)(z - 10)$

RETEACHING 11–9

1. **General**
   $m(ax + by)(ax - by)$
   $m(a^2x^2 - axby + axby - b^2y^2)$
   $m(a^2x^2 - b^2y^2)$
   $ma^2x^2 - mb^2y^2$
   Specific
   $5(2x + 4)(2x - 4)$
   $5(4x^2 - 8x + 8x - 16)$
   $5(4x^2 - 16)$
   $20x^2 - 80$
2. **General**
   $m(x + ay)(x + by)$
   $m(x^2 + bxy + axy + aby^2)$
   $m[x^2 + (b + a)xy + aby^2]$
   $mx^2 + m(b + a)xy + maby^2$
   Specific
   $4(x + 3y)(x + 2y)$
   $4(x^2 + 2xy + 3xy + 6y^2)$
   $4(x^2 + 5xy + 6y^2)$
   $4x^2 + 20xy + 24y^2$

RETEACHING 11–10

1. $-; -$
2. $+; +$
3. $-; +$
4. $-; +$
5. $+; -$
6. $-; +$
7. $(2x + 3)(2x + 1)$
8. $(3x - 4)(2x - 1)$
9. $(4x + 2)(2x - 3)$
10. $(3x - 4)(3x + 2)$
11. $(5x + 3)(3x + 1)$
12. $(4x - 3)(2x + 1)$
13. $(3x - 4)(3x - 2)$
14. $(3x - 1)(5x + 2)$
15. $(2x + 5)(3x - 10)$
16. $(2x - 7)(3x + 2)$
17. $(6x - 3)(x + 4)$
18. $(5x + 5)(2x - 5)$

RETEACHING 12–1

Ordered pairs may vary for Exercises 1–3; sample given.

1. $(0, 3)$

x	y
2	7
1	4
0	3
-1	4
-2	7

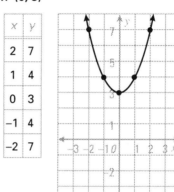

2. $(0, 2)$

x	y
2	-2
1	1
0	2
-1	1
-2	?

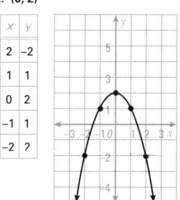

3. $(0, 0)$

x	y
2	8
1	2
0	0
-1	2
-2	8

RETEACHING 12–2

1. Vertex: (–1, 2)
   Axis of symmetry: $x = -1$

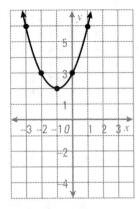

2. Vertex: (0, 3)
   Axis of symmetry: $x = 0$

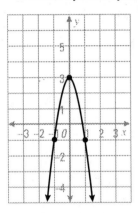

3. Vertex: (–1, –4)
   Axis of symmetry: $x = -1$

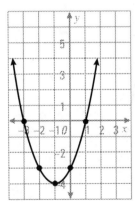

RETEACHING 12–3

1. No, because some *x*-values have more than one *y*-value.
2. Yes, because there is only one *y*-value for each *x*-value.
3. No, because some *x*-values have more than one *y*-value.
4. Yes, because there is only one *y*-value for each *x*-value.

RETEACHING 12–4

1. $x = 9, x = -9$ 2. $x = 6, x = -1$
3. $x = 1$ 4. $x = 3, x = -9$
5. $x = -5, x = 3$ 6. $x = 7, x = -5$
7. $x = 8, x = -7$ 8. $x = 3, x = -2$
9. $x = 0, x = -\frac{1}{2}$ 10. No solution
11. $x = 0, x = 3$ 12. $x = -9, x = 1$
13. $x = 0, x = -10$ 14. $x = -4, x = 4$

RETEACHING 12–5

1. $x^2 + 8x + 16$ 2. $x^2 - 4x + 4$
3. $x^2 + 10x + 25$ 4. $x^2 + 2x + 1$
5. $x^2 - 12x + 36$ 6. $x^2 - 14x + 49$
7. $x = -7, x = 1$ 8. $x = -1, x = 5$
9. $x = -1, x = 17$ 10. $x = -1, x = -9$
11. $x = 1, x = 11$ 12. $x = 5, x = -9$
13. $x = -8, x = -2$ 14. $x = -11, x = -1$
15. $x = -22, x = -2$ 16. $x = 11, x = -3$

RETEACHING 12–6

1. $x = 5, x = 2$ 2. $x = \frac{5}{3}, x = -1$
3. $x = -\frac{2}{5}, x = 1$ 4. $x = -10$
5. $x = 6, x = -2$ 6. $x = -2, x = -3$
7. $x = -5 \pm \sqrt{37}$ 8. $x = 3 \pm \sqrt{11}$
9. $x = 7 \pm \sqrt{61}$ 10. $x = -2 \pm \sqrt{5}$
11. $x = 3, x = -4$ 12. $x = 7 \pm 2\sqrt{6}$
13. $x = -15$ 14. $x = -2 \pm \sqrt{2}$

RETEACHING 12–7

1. $\sqrt{13} \approx 3.6$ 2. $\sqrt{26} \approx 5.1$
3. $\sqrt{29} \approx 5.4$ 4. $\sqrt{2} \approx 1.4$
5. $\sqrt{169} = 13$ 6. $\sqrt{5} \approx 2.2$
7. $\sqrt{68} \approx 8.2$ 8. $\sqrt{85} \approx 9.2$
9. $\sqrt{82} \approx 9.1$ 10. (3, 4)
11. (5, 3)   12. (–1, 2)
13. (–2, 4)   14. (1, 1)
15. (–2, –2)   16. (4, –4)
17. (–6, –1)   18. (–2, 1)

RETEACHING 12–8

1. a. 1.75 seconds;   b. 49 feet
2. 8 seconds
3. About 31.9 miles
4. About 7.4 seconds
5. 36 feet

RETEACHING 13–1

1. $(x - 3)^2 + (y + 4)^2 = 25$
2. $(x + 5)^2 + y^2 = 9$
3. $x^2 + y^2 = 36$
4. $r = 12$; center $(0, 0)$
5. $r = \sqrt{21}$; center $(3, -6)$
6. $r = \sqrt{34}$; center $(-4, -5)$
7. $r = \sqrt{18}$; center $(2, 4)$
8. $r = 25$; center $(0, 0)$
9. $r = \sqrt{48}$; center $(-5, 6)$

RETEACHING 13–2

1. $F (0, -3)$; $D (y = 3)$
2. $F (0, \frac{5}{4})$; $D (y = -\frac{5}{4})$
3. $F (0, -6)$; $D (y = 6)$
4. $F (0, 4)$; $D (y = -4)$
5. $F (0, -\frac{13}{4})$; $D (y = \frac{13}{4})$
6. $F (0, 1)$; $D (y = -1)$
7. $x^2 = -28y$
8. $x^2 = 32y$
9. $x^2 = 8y$
10. $x^2 = -36y$
11. $x^2 = -20y$
12. $x^2 = -\frac{4}{3} y$

RETEACHING 13–3

1. Circle   2. Parabola   3. Triangle   4. Square
5. Rectangle   6. Circle   7. Rectangle
8. Parallelogram   9. Triangle   10. Pentagon
11. Ellipse   12. Rectangle

RETEACHING 13–4

1. $12 x^2 + 16y^2 = 192$
2. $9 x^2 + 25y^2 = 225$
3. $11 x^2 + 36y^2 = 396$
4. $45x^2 + 49y^2 = 2{,}205$
5. $16 x^2 + 25y^2 = 400$
6. $13 x^2 + 49y^2 = 637$
7. $4x^2 - 16y^2 = 64$
8. $16 x^2 - 9y^2 = 144$
9. $16 x^2 - 36y^2 = 576$
10. $64 x^2 - 25y^2 = 1{,}600$
11. $49 x^2 - 81y^2 = 3{,}969$
12. $25 x^2 - 49y^2 = 1{,}225$

RETEACHING 13–5

1. $y = 0.5x$ 2. $y = 0.48x$ 3. $y = 0.2x$
4. $y = 0.4x$ 5. $y = 0.8x$ 6. $y = 0.625x$ 7. 96
g   8. 120 ft   9. 416 mi   10. 30 lb

RETEACHING 13–6

1. $y = \frac{12}{x}$
2. $y = \frac{72}{x}$
3. $y = \frac{140}{x}$
4. $y = \frac{90}{x}$
5. $y = \frac{45}{x}$
6. $y = \frac{222}{x}$
7. 80 ohms
8. $3\frac{1}{3}$ h

RETEACHING 13–7

1.

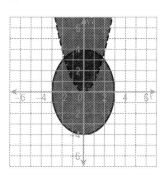

2.

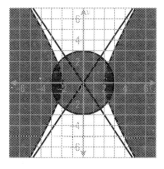

3.

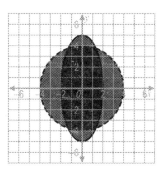

RETEACHING 13–8

1. 4 %   2. 4 mi/h   3. 2 ft   4. 35 mi/h

RETEACHING 14–1

1. tan D: $1\frac{1}{3}$

   sin E: $\frac{3}{5}$

   cos E: $\frac{4}{5}$

   cos D: $\frac{3}{5}$

2. tan G: $2\frac{2}{5}$

   sin I: $\frac{5}{13}$

   sin G: $\frac{12}{13}$

   cos I: $\frac{12}{13}$

3. cos L: $\frac{3}{5}$

   sin J: $\frac{3}{5}$

   sin L: $\frac{4}{5}$

   tan J: $\frac{3}{4}$

4. tan O: $1\frac{7}{8}$

   sin O: $\frac{15}{17}$

   tan N: $\frac{8}{15}$

   cos N: $\frac{15}{17}$

RETEACHING 14–2

1. $\overline{DF}$: 6.7 ft

   $m\angle D$: 42°

   $m\angle E$: 48°

2. $m\angle H$: 35°

   $\overline{GI}$: 2.9 cm

   $\overline{GH}$: 4.1 cm

3. $\overline{JK}$: 7.3 yd

   $\overline{JL}$: 2.1 yd

   $m\angle K$: 17°

4. $m\angle O$: 27°

   $m\angle N$: 63°

   $\overline{ON}$: 15.7

RETEACHING 14–3

1. 321.4 ft   2. 142.8 ft   3. 43.3 m   4. 8.2 ft
5. 21 ft   6. 8,267.9 ft   7. 2,291.6 m

RETEACHING 14–4

1. $\frac{1}{2}$

2. $\frac{\sqrt{3}}{2}$

3. $\frac{\sqrt{2}}{2}$

4. $-\frac{\sqrt{2}}{2}$

5. $\frac{1}{2}$

6. $-\frac{\sqrt{3}}{2}$

7. $-\frac{\sqrt{2}}{2}$

8. $\frac{\sqrt{3}}{2}$

9. $\frac{\sqrt{3}}{2}$

RETEACHING 14–5

1. Period: 72°
   Amplitude: 3
   Position: Down 2 units
2. Period: 120°
   Amplitude: 5
   Position: Up 1 unit
3. Period: 90°
   Amplitude: 3
   Position: Down 3 units
4. Period: 240°
   Amplitude: 4
   Position: Up 5 units

RETEACHING 14–6

Strategies will vary for Exercises 1–7.
1. 5.7 in.
2. Carter is 13. Carrie is 18.
3. José, Huang, Sam
4. 1,841.6 m
5. 57.1 ft
6. 300 handshakes
7. 10 mi

ENRICHMENT 1–1

1. 10   2. 28   3. 55   4. 91

5. $\frac{1}{2}(n+1)(n+2)$ 6. $n+2$

7. $(n+2)\cdot\frac{1}{2}n(n+1)$

8. The numbers at the ends of each chain are the same.

9. The numbers at the ends will be 3 and 4. Yes, it is always true.

10. n must be equal to 1 or even.

ENRICHMENT 1–2

1. They get closer to ϕ, alternating between being a little greater and a little less.

2. $\frac{89}{55}$

3. The result gets closer and closer to ϕ, starting with 1.414 . . .

4. 9 times.

Check students' drawings for Exercises 5–7.

ENRICHMENT 1–3

1. Set A = {2, 2, 23}
   Set B = {3, 7, 23}
   Set C = {2, 3, 23}
   GCF = 23
   LCM = 1,932

2. Set A = {5, 5, 7}
   Set B = {2, 3, 5, 13}
   Set C = {5, 97}
   GCF = 5
   LCM = 1,324,050

3. Set A = {3, 3, 11}
   Set B = {2, 3, 5, 11}
   Set C = {2, 3, 7, 11}
   GCF = 33
   LCM = 6,930

4. Set A = {2, 5, 7, 7}
   Set B = {3, 5, 7, 13}
   Set C = {5, 7, 11, 11}
   GCF = 35
   LCM = 2,312,310

5. Set A = {2, 5, 11, 17}
   Set B = {2, 2, 2, 3, 17}
   Set C = {2, 2, 17, 23}
   GCF = 34
   LCM = 516,120

6. Set A = {2, 2, 11, 13, 23}
   Set B = {5, 11, 13, 41}
   Set C = {11, 13, 19, 19}
   GCF = 143
   LCM = 973,609,780

ENRICHMENT 1–4

1. 0 ft   2. $\frac{1}{8}$ ft   3. $\frac{7}{24}$ ft   4. $\frac{13}{24}$ ft

5. $1\frac{1}{24}$ ft   6. $\frac{1}{2}$ ft   7. $\frac{3}{8}$ ft   8. $\frac{5}{24}$ ft

9. $-\frac{1}{24}$ ft   10. $-\frac{13}{24}$ ft

11. $\frac{1}{10}$ ft; the center of gravity is one-tenth of a foot to the left of the edge of the table. So, the stack is stable and will not topple. Students might enjoy building the stack to check.

ENRICHMENT 1–5

1. $\frac{6,729}{13,458}$ 2. $\frac{5,823}{17,469}$ 3. $\frac{3,942}{15,768}$ 4. $\frac{2,697}{13,485}$

5. $\frac{2,943}{17,658}$ 6. $\frac{2,394}{16,758}$ 7. $\frac{3,187}{25,496}$ 8. $\frac{6,381}{57,429}$

9. $96\frac{2,148}{537}$ 10. $96\frac{1,752}{438}$ 11. $96\frac{1,428}{357}$

12. $94\frac{1,578}{263}$ 13. $91\frac{7,524}{836}$ 14. $91\frac{5,823}{647}$

15. $91\frac{5,742}{638}$ 16. $82\frac{3,546}{197}$ 17. $81\frac{7,524}{396}$

18. $81\frac{5,643}{297}$ 19. $3\frac{69,258}{714}$

ENRICHMENT 1–6

1.

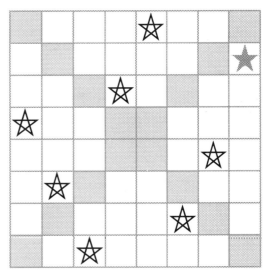

2. 7 more solutions, 3 through rotation and 4 more through reflection

3.

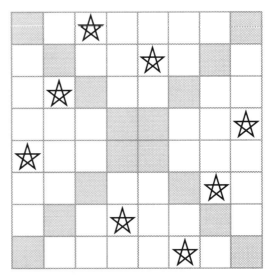

4. 3 more solutions; this solution has rotational symmetry of order 2 so there are fewer new solutions through rotation and reflection

ENRICHMENT 1-7

1. $3 \cdot 4^2 \cdot 6$
2. $3^4 \cdot 6$
3. 1 square, 2 octagons
4. 3 equilateral triangles, 2 squares
5. They are 6^3, 4^4, and 3^6. The second is made of squares; the third of equilateral triangles.

ENRICHMENT 1-8

1. $2^{2^0} + 1$ 3.0×10^0 3
2. $2^{2^1} + 1$ 5.0×10^0 5
3. $2^{2^2} + 1$ 1.7×10^1 17
4. $2^{2^3} + 1$ 2.57×10^2 257
5. $2^{2^4} + 1$ 6.55×10^4 65,537
6. $2^{2^5} + 1$ 4.29×10^9 4,294,967,297
7. $2^{2^6} + 1$ 1.84×10^{19} 18,446,744,073, 709,551,617
8. 6,700,417
9. 67,280,421,310,721

ENRICHMENT 1-9

1. 800–350–323–620–602–152–143–440
2. 12 00–570–525–10 20–372–345–840–804–174–165–660

CALCULATOR 1-3

1. +   2. ×   3. +   4. ×   5. $2 \geq x \geq -2$
6. $6 \leq x < 3$ 7. $-3 \leq x < 7$
8. The section of the graph that is part of both inequalities is graphed at $y = 2$.

COMPUTER 1-8

1. 3.99704×10^{15}
   9.4048×10^{14}
   3.35046×10^{14}
   5.2902×10^{14}
2. 30 N = A * 9.461E+12
   40 PRINT "THE DISTANCE IN KILOMETERS IS "; N
3. 1.51376E+15
4. 50 PRINT "DO YOU WANT TO COMPUTE ANOTHER? TYPE Y OR N."
   70 IF X$ = "Y" THEN GOTO 10
5. 4.3E+23

6. 2.3E–13
7. 5.28E–20

ENRICHMENT 2-1

1.

2.

3.

4.

5.

6.

7.

8.

9.

10.

11.

ENRICHMENT 2-2

Answers will vary for Exercises 1–6.

ENRICHMENT 2-3

1. 6   2. 6   3. –7   4. –6
5. 0   6. –1   7. 0   8. 3

9.

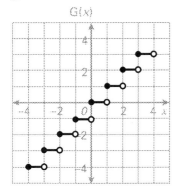

10.

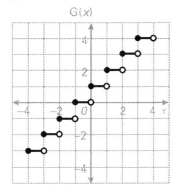

11.

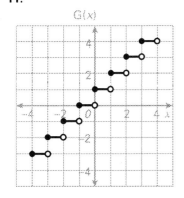

12.

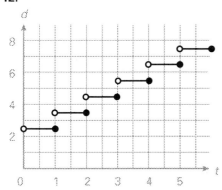

13. Its graph looks like a series of steps.

ENRICHMENT 2–4

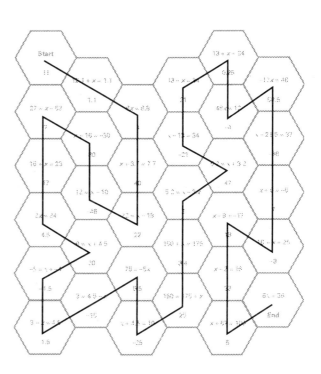

ENRICHMENT 2–5

1. C   2. A   3. B   4. D   5. B   6. A
7. B   8. C   9. D   10. B

ENRICHMENT 2–6

1. 20 sq units   2. 32 sq units
3. 25 sq units   4. 14 sq units
5. 34 sq units   6. 42 sq units

ENRICHMENT 2–7

1. −5, −4, −3   2. 8, 9   3. 23, 24, 25
4. 47, 48   5. 203, 205, 207
6. −23, −21, −19, −17   7. 34, 36
8. −8, −6, −4   9. 4, 6   10. 6, 8, 10, 12

ENRICHMENT 2–8

1. 16   36   64   81
   64   64   49   16
2. A two-digit square ends in 1, 4, 5, 6, or 9. So, the number in the lower row must begin with one of these digits.
3. 100, 121, 144, 169, 196, 225, 256, 289, 324, 361, 400, 441, 484, 529, 576, 625, 676, 729, 784, 841, 900, 961

4. 0, 1, 4, 5, 6, or 9
5. 144, 169, 196, and 441
6.

144	529	729	169	441	841	144
484	256	256	676	400	400	400
441	961	961	961	100	100	100

441	841	121	121	361	961
484	484	289	256	676	676
144	144	196	169	169	169

ENRICHMENT 2–9

Estimates will vary for Exercises 1–6.

7. 45 sq units   8. 36 sq units   9. 52 sq units

ENRICHMENT 2–10

1.

Peg A	Peg B	Peg C
1 2		
2	1	
	1	2
		1 2

Peg A	Peg B	Peg C
1 2		
2		1
	2	1
	1 2	

2.

Peg A	Peg B	Peg C
1 2 3		
2 3		1
3	2	1
3	1 2	
	1 2	3
1	2	3
1		2 3
		1 2 3

Other solutions are possible.

COMPUTER 2–1

1. 1; 1; 2; 3; 5; 8; 13; 21; 34; 55; 89; 144; 233; 377; 610; 987; 1,597; 2,584; 4,181; 6,765
2. 10 DIM N(40); 20 FOR I = 1 TO 40
3. The program prints 1.
4. The program prints 1.
5. It adds N(17) + N(16).
6. 1, 1.5, 1.6, 1.615385, 1.617647, 1.617977, 1.618026, 1.618033, 1.618034, 1.618034
7. 1.618033989; this is close to the ratio of Fibonacci terms.

CALCULATOR 2–9

1. 188.5833333   2. 191.3076923

ENRICHMENT

1.

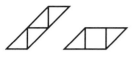

2. *Possible answer:*
   If the squares are 1 in. on a side, the total area of the 14 pieces is 28 sq in. And, 28 is not a square number.
3. *Check students' figures.*
4.

5. *There are eight possible solutions.*

ENRICHMENT 3–2

1. 72°, 108° 2. 144°, 36° 3. 60°, 120°
4. 120°, 60° 5. 36°, 144° 6. 72°, 108°
7. 108°, 72° 8. 144°, 36° 9. 30°, 150°
10. 60°, 120° 11. 90°, 90° 12. 120°, 60°
13. 150°, 30°
14. Exterior angles are successive multiples of 360° ÷ *n*.
15. There are 3 star polygons. Exterior angles are 40°, 80°, 120°, and 160°.

ENRICHMENT 3–3

1. *Data will vary, depending on the angles students choose.*
2. $n = \dfrac{360°}{\theta} - 1$

ENRICHMENT 3–4

1. 6   2. 96   3. 8   4. 128

ENRICHMENT 3–5

1. $\triangle A$: three 60° angles, three 3-unit sides; $\triangle$s *B* and *C*: 30-60-90, 2-unit hypotenuse and 1-unit shorter leg; $\triangle$s *D* and *E*: 30-60-90, 3-unit longer leg
2. *Check students' figures.*
3.

4.

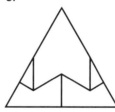

5.

ENRICHMENT 3–6

1. 2 ways

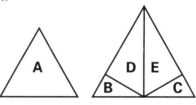

2. 14 ways

3. **14**   4. **42**

5. **132**

$D_7 + D_3D_6 + D_4D_5 + D_5D_4 + D_6D_3 + D_7$

6. **429**

$D_8 + D_3D_7 + D_4D_6 + D_5D_5 + D_6D_4 + D_7D_3 + D_8$

7. **1,430**

$D_9 + D_3D_8 + D_4D_7 + D_5D_6 + D_6D_5 + D_7D_4 + D_8D_3 + D_9$

COMPUTER 3–5

1. **SETH 0**   2. **SETH 270**
3. **SETH 225**   4. **SETH 45**
6. **Before the last line, type SETH 90.**
7. **FD 60 PU; HOME PD SETH 45 FD 60 PU; HOME PD SETH 90 FD 60 PU; HOME PD SETH 135 FD 60 PU; HOME PD SETH 180 FD 60 PU; HOME PD SETH 225 FD 60 PU; HOME PD SETH 270 FD 60 PU; HOME PD SETH 315 FD 60**

CALCULATOR 3–6

1. **The graph of an equation in the form $y = x^2 + c$ is a parabola. It intersects the x-axis at c.**
2. **The graph of $n \log X$ opens upward to the right if n is +, downward to the right if n is –.**
3. **The graph of $\ln ax$ is in Q1 if +ln, +a; in Q4 if –ln, +a; Q3 if –ln, –a; in Q2 if +ln, –a.**

ENRICHMENT 3–7

1.

2.
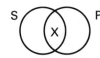

3. **All P is S.**
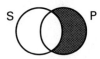

4. **No P is S.**

5. **Some P is S.**

6. **Some P is not S.**
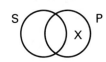

7. **No S is P $\leftrightarrow$ No P is S**

ENRICHMENT 3–8

Examples will vary for Exercises 1–6.

ENRICHMENT 3–9

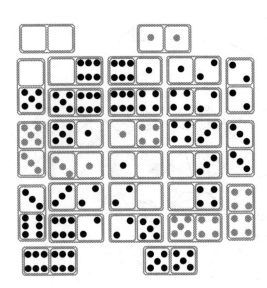

ENRICHMENT 4–1

1. **1, 4, 11, 24, 45**
2.

Many different solutions are possible for Exercises 3–4.
Two solutions are shown.

3.

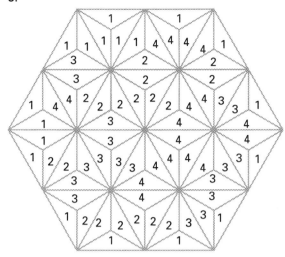

4.

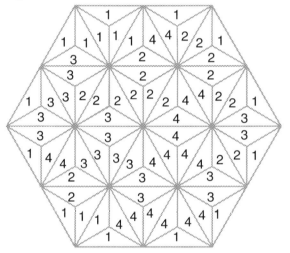

ENRICHMENT 4–2

1. *Check students' constructions.*
2. The triangle is tangent to the inner circle at the three points of intersection.

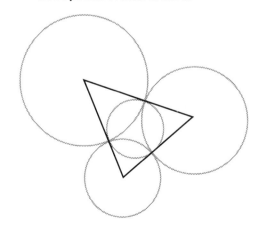

3.

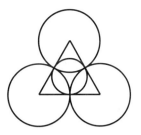

4. They intersect at a common point.
5. A triangle similar to the original triangle.
6.

7. No, the figures are different.

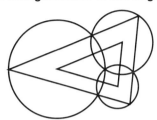

ENRICHMENT 4–3

1. 2. right
   3. SAS
   4. ∠C

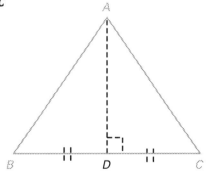

2. The midpoint of $\overline{BC}$ is not always the same point as the foot of the perpendicular from vertex A.

3.

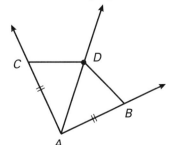

6. The ray which bisects ∠A does not necessarily contain the point *D*.

ENRICHMENT 4–4

1. Segment *OD* divides it into two parts of equal area; area of △*BOD* equals area of △*DOC*.
2. area △*BOF* = area △*FOA*; area △*AOE* = area △*EOC*
3. Use the same reasoning again, with △*ABC* and segment *EB*.
4. In $2y + z = z + 2x$, subtract z from both sides. Then, divide through by 0. Thus, $y = x$. Use △*ABC* with segment *AD* to get $2z + x = x + 2y$. This will give $z = y$. Thus $x = y = z$.
5. *AO* must be twice *OD*.
6. Use the same reasoning as in Exercise 5 two more times, once with △*BEA* and again with △*CFA*.

ENRICHMENT 4–5

1. 45–47, 43–45, 64–44–46, 24–44, 47–45–43, 42–44
2. 55–53–33, 35–55, 65–45, 44–46, 33–35, 25–45, 46–44
3. 34–36, 15–35, 54–56, 75–55, 36–34–54–52, 42–44, 56–54–34, 24–44, 45–43, 33–53, 52–54, 64–44
   or 34–14, 43–23, 44–46, 54–56–36–34, 75–55, 15–13–33–35, 25–45–65–63–43, 42–44

ENRICHMENT 4–6

1.	0	3	4	7		2.	3	5	14	22
3.	7	6	21	34		4.	13	7	30	50
5.	22	8	40	70		6.	34	9	52	95
7.	50	10	65	125						

8. d   9. f   10. b   11. a   12. g   13. e
14. c

ENRICHMENT 4–7

1. 5 bands
2. 12 rhombuses
3. Numbering outward from the center, the 1st and 5th bands contain 30°–150° rhombuses; the 2nd and 4th bands contain 60°–120° rhombuses; and the 3rd band contains 90°–90° rhombuses (squares).

4. 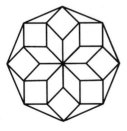   5.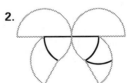

6.

7. $n(\frac{n}{2} - 1)$

8. No, for *n* odd, the total is $n(n - 1)/2$. And, the first band of rhombuses overlaps in the center so, strictly speaking, these are not "tessellations." *Examples will vary.*

ENRICHMENT 4–8

1. 3. $\overline{DY}$; $\overline{CY}$
   4. *DYB*
   5. $\overline{YB}$
   6. *CB*

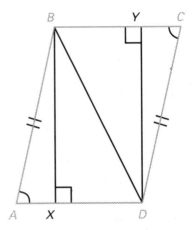

2.

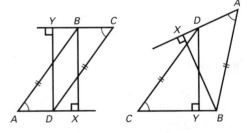

The proof is valid for the middle case, but not for the other two.

3. The proof is not true if *X* is on the quadrilateral and *Y* is not, or vice versa. It is true if both *X* and *Y* are either on, or off, the quadrilateral.

ENRICHMENT 4–9

1.   2.

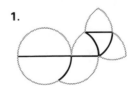

3.

4.

5.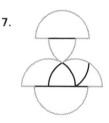

6.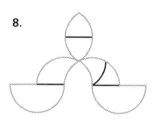

7.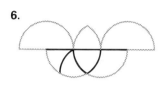

8.

9.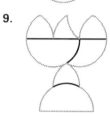

10. Most people find the circular tangram puzzles easier to solve, possibly because some of the pieces have more distinct shapes.

ENRICHMENT 4–10

1. *Check students' work.*

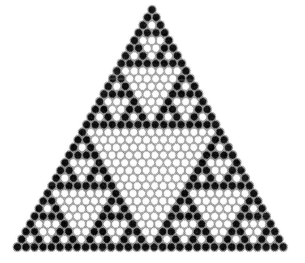

2. Sierpinski's triangle
3. Alternating shaded and unshaded equilateral triangles

CALCULATOR 4–2

1. Congruent, SAS
2. Congruent, SAS
3. Not congruent
4. Congruent, SAS

COMPUTER 4–8

3. Both are parallelograms; corresponding sides are equal in measure.
4. Turtle is not shown in second drawing; the measures of the angles are different.
5. *Programs will vary. Possible answer:* REPEAT 2[FD 50 RT 105 FD 80 RT 75]
6. Parallelogram-sides theorem
7. Make the forward command the same number each time.
8. *Programs will vary. Possible answer:* REPEAT 2[FD 70 RT 120 FD 70 RT 60]
9. yes

ENRICHMENT 5–1

1. Nick: $200; Alice: $300
2. Tony: $1,350; Angela: $900; Kiko: $750
3. $2,912.58; $4,047.75; $3,769.51; $2,426.62; $4,726.19; $2,690.24; $5,186.10; $4,240.86

ENRICHMENT 5–2

1. Areas: 65 sq units; 64 sq units
   Explanation: The pieces actually overlap along the diagonal lines.
2. Areas: 64 sq units; 63 sq units
   Explanation: The rectangle actually has a height of $9\frac{1}{7}$ units.
3. Areas: 64 sq units; 63 sq units
   Explanation: There is a slight overlap along the diagonal.
4. Areas: 121 sq units; 119 sq units
   Explanation: The grid lines of sections A and B do not line up with those of section C.

ENRICHMENT 5–3

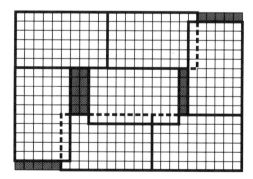

The maximum is 25 in.²
There are many different arrangements that will give the maximum coverage.

ENRICHMENT 5–4

1.

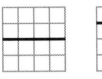

2.

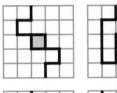

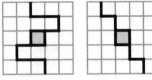

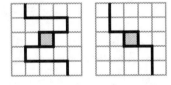

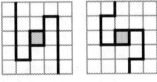

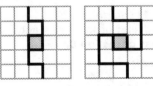

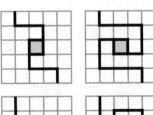

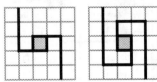

3.

4.

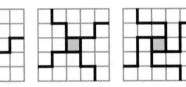

ENRICHMENT 5–5

1.

2.

3.

4.

5.

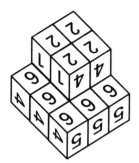

6.

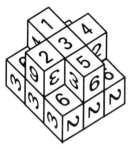

7. D   8. C   9. A   10. E   11. B

ENRICHMENT 5–6

1. *Check students' models.*
2. 6 octagons and 8 regular hexagons
3. *Check students' models.*
4. 6 octagons and 8 equilateral triangles
5. 241.1 in.^{2}
6. 291.9 in.^{2}

ENRICHMENT 5–7

1.

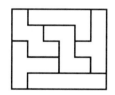   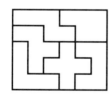

Many solutions are possible.
2. *Many solutions are possible.*
3. *Answers will vary.*

ENRICHMENT 5–8

	I	N	T	E	R	S	E	C	T	I	N	G		T	
				A		D		W						R	
		V		L		G	E	O	M	E	T	R	Y		
	M	E	A	S	U	R	E				Q		E		
		R		C				O		U		V			
		T		P	I		P	E	N	T	A	G	O	N	
E		E		D		O		E		T		L			N
S	I	X		A	N	G	L	E		F	I	G	U	R	E
T		I		E		Y			O		T		E		
I		N		P		H			N		I		T		
M		V	E	R	T	E	X		P		F	O	U	R	
A		E		E		D		R		N		I			
T		R		P	Y	R	A	M	I	D				H	
E		S				O			S		N	O	T		
S	P	H	E	R	E		N	O	R	M	A	L			

ANEMOMETER

CALCULATOR 5–2

1. 345 m^2
2. 756 ft^2
3. 553 cm^2
4. 628 yd^2

COMPUTER 5–7

1. 1, 1.5, 2, 2.5, 3, 3.5, 4, 4.5, 5, 5.5, 6, 6.5, 7, 7.5, 8, 8.5, 9, 9.5, 10
2. The volume of a cylinder with a volume of 750; 750 = 3.14 * R^2 * H
3. R = 5, H = 9.55414
4. 30 FOR R = 4.5 TO 5.5 STEP .1
5. R = 4.9 cm; H = 9.9 cm
6. Change line 40 to LET H = 250/(3.14 * R^2)

ENRICHMENT 6–1

1. 5 km/hr
2. 12.5 yd/sec
3. 62,500 mi/hr
4. 30 mi/hr
5. 4 m/sec
6. 750 mi/hr
7. 1, 5, 2, 4, 6, 3
(Converting to mi/hr, 5 km/hr ≈ 3, 12.5 yd/sec ≈ 25.6, 4 m/sec ≈ 8.6.)
8. *Answers will vary.*

ENRICHMENT 6–2

1. $\dfrac{x}{-3} + \dfrac{y}{5} = 1$

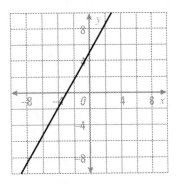

2. $\dfrac{x}{2} + \dfrac{y}{6} = 1$

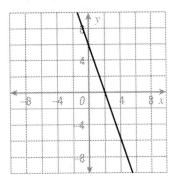

3. $\dfrac{x}{4} + \dfrac{y}{-5} = 1$

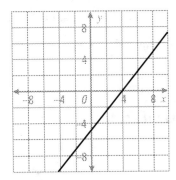

4. $\dfrac{x}{-1} + \dfrac{y}{-8} = 1$

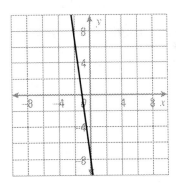

5. $\dfrac{x}{-9} + \dfrac{y}{4} = 1$

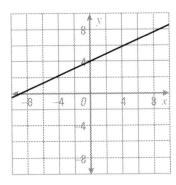

6. $\dfrac{x}{2} + \dfrac{y}{-7} = 1$

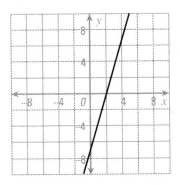

ENRICHMENT 6–3

Equations will vary for Exercises 1–3; graphs will show two parallel lines.

4. If the coefficients of two equations satisfy the proportion $A_1 : B_1 = A_2 : B_2$, their graphs are parallel.

Equations will vary for Exercises 5–7; graphs will show two perpendicular lines.

8. If the coefficients of two equations satisfy the proportion $A_1 : B_1 = -B_2 : A_2$, their graphs are perpendicular.

ENRICHMENT 6–4

1. $\dfrac{x}{6} + \dfrac{y}{4} + \dfrac{z}{5} = 1$

2. $\dfrac{x}{3} + \dfrac{y}{5} + \dfrac{z}{3} = 1$

3. $\dfrac{x}{4} + \dfrac{y}{3} = 1$

4. $\dfrac{x}{4} + \dfrac{y}{5} + \dfrac{z}{4} = 1$

5. $\dfrac{y}{3} + \dfrac{z}{5} = 1$

6. $\dfrac{x}{6} + \dfrac{y}{3} + \dfrac{z}{3} = 1$

7. $x = 3$

8. $z = -1$

ENRICHMENT 6–5

1. $y = -0.5x + k$

2. $y = kx + 6$

3. $y = 3x + k$

4. $y + 6 = k(x - 4)$

5. $y - 4 = k(x + 2)$

6. $y + 6 = k(x + 6)$

ENRICHMENT 6–6

1.

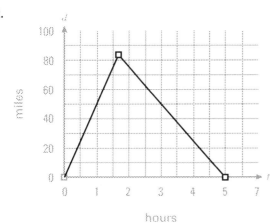

2.

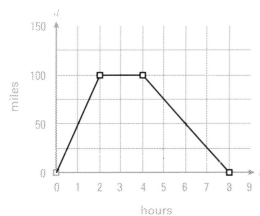

3.

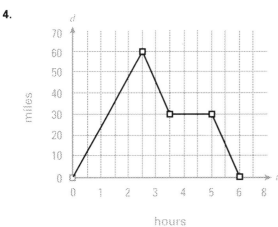

4.

ENRICHMENT 6–7

1. $P = (0, 4.5)$

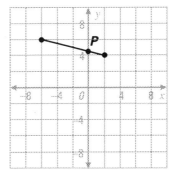

2. $P = (3.5, -2)$

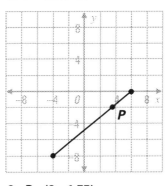

3. $P = (2, -1.75)$

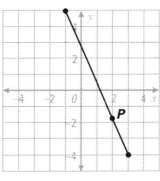

4. $P = (0.75, 0.5)$

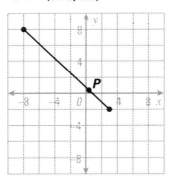

Enrichment

ENRICHMENT 6–8

1. (3, 21)
2. (12, 12)
3. (0, 0)
4. (12, –12)
5. (3, –21)
6. (3, 21)
7. (9, –21)
8. (0, –12)
9. (12, 0)
10. (0, 12)
11. (9, 21)
12. (9, –21)

Pattern on the graph looks like this:

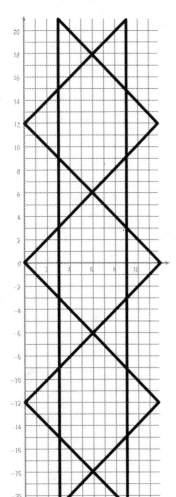

ENRICHMENT 6–9

1. 3 hours
2. 6 days
3. 15 minutes
4. 24 hours
5. 2 hours
6. Tanya: 30 hours; Rob: 15 hours

ENRICHMENT 6–10

1.

4	7	10	13	**16**	19	22	25	28	31
7	12	17	**22**	27	32	37	42	47	52
10	17	**24**	31	38	45	52	59	66	73
13	**22**	31	40	49	58	67	76	85	94
16	27	38	49	60	71	82	93	104	115
19	32	45	58	71	84	97	110	123	136
22	37	52	67	82	97	112	127	142	157
25	42	59	76	93	110	127	144	161	178

2. *Answers will vary.*
3. *Answers will vary.*

ENRICHMENT 6–11

1. $y \le 2$; $y \ge -3$; $y \le \frac{5}{2}x + 12$; $y \le -\frac{5}{2}x + \frac{9}{2}$
2. $y \le -x + 1$; $y \ge \frac{1}{3}x - 3$; $y \ge -9x - 31$
3. $y \le 6$; $y \ge 4$; $y \le -2$; $y \ge -4$; $x \ge -5$; $x \le -2$; $x \ge 1$; $x \le 4$
4. $y \le 5$; $y \ge -5$; $y \ge -x - 2$; $y \le x + 2$; $y \ge x - 2$; $y \le -x + 2$

Answers will vary for Exercises 5–6.

ENRICHMENT 6–12

1. 3 different right triangles, 2 large congruent equilateral triangles, 2 smaller congruent equilateral triangles, 2 congruent trapezoids
2. *Check students' work.*
3.

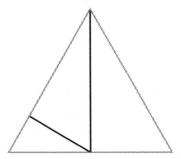

4.

CALCULATOR 6–10

1. $(4, -1)$

$$D = \begin{bmatrix} 3 & 4 \\ 2 & 3 \end{bmatrix} \qquad D_x = \begin{bmatrix} 8 & 4 \\ 5 & 3 \end{bmatrix} \qquad D_y = \begin{bmatrix} 3 & 8 \\ 2 & 5 \end{bmatrix}$$

2. $(2, 2)$

$$D = \begin{bmatrix} 3 & -1 \\ 1 & 2 \end{bmatrix} \qquad D_x = \begin{bmatrix} 4 & -1 \\ 6 & 2 \end{bmatrix} \qquad D_y = \begin{bmatrix} 3 & 4 \\ 1 & 6 \end{bmatrix}$$

3. $(3, -1)$

$$D = \begin{bmatrix} 2 & -1 \\ 1 & 2 \end{bmatrix} \qquad D_x = \begin{bmatrix} 7 & -1 \\ 1 & 2 \end{bmatrix} \qquad D_y = \begin{bmatrix} 2 & 7 \\ 1 & 1 \end{bmatrix}$$

4. $(4, 2)$

$$D = \begin{bmatrix} 1 & -1 \\ 1 & 1 \end{bmatrix} \qquad D_x = \begin{bmatrix} 2 & -1 \\ 6 & 1 \end{bmatrix} \qquad D_y = \begin{bmatrix} 1 & 2 \\ 1 & 6 \end{bmatrix}$$

5. $(-2, 4)$

$$D = \begin{bmatrix} 3 & 2 \\ -2 & 1 \end{bmatrix} \qquad D_x = \begin{bmatrix} 2 & 2 \\ 8 & 1 \end{bmatrix} \qquad D_y = \begin{bmatrix} 3 & 2 \\ -2 & 8 \end{bmatrix}$$

6. $(2, -1)$

$$D = \begin{bmatrix} 3 & 4 \\ 2 & -1 \end{bmatrix} \qquad D_x = \begin{bmatrix} 2 & 4 \\ 5 & -1 \end{bmatrix} \qquad D_y = \begin{bmatrix} 3 & 2 \\ 2 & 5 \end{bmatrix}$$

COMPUTER 6–11

1. $(0, 1)$, $(3, 0)$, $(3, 1)$, $(3, 2)$
2. $(-3, 2)$, $(-3, 1)$, $(-3, 0)$, $(-1, 1)$
3. $(0, -2)$, $(0, -1)$, $(0, 0)$, $(1, -2)$, $(1, -1)$
4. Change E2: @C2<=3 and F2: @D2>=0
5. They are not in the solution of $y < 2x + 1$ and $y \geq x - 2$
6. Region II
8. *Check students' spreadsheets and graphs.*

ENRICHMENT 7–1

1. 63 bushels 2. $600 3. 1,430 reams
4. 162 appliances 5. 125 slabs

ENRICHMENT 7–2

Check students' work for Exercises 1–3.

ENRICHMENT 7–3

1. 2 × 2 square minus 1 unit square

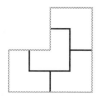

2. 2 × 3 rectangle minus 1 unit square

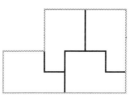

3. 2 × 3 rectangle minus 2 unit squares

4. 60°, 120°, 60°, 120°

5. 90°, 90°, 60°, 120°

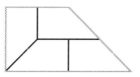

6. 90°, 90°, 45°, 135°

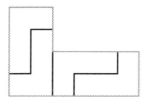

7.

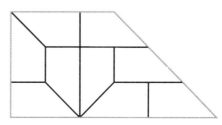

8.

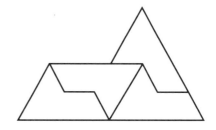

ENRICHMENT 7–4

1.

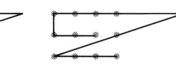

2.

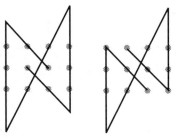

3.

4.

ENRICHMENT 7–5

1. *Many correct answers are possible.*

2.

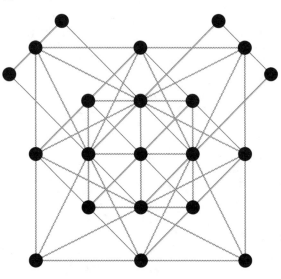

ENRICHMENT 7–6

1. *Check students' work.*

2. None

3.

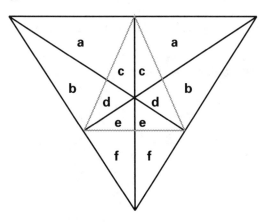

4. *Check students' work.*

5. *Check students' work.*

6. Any point on an angle bisector is equidistant from the two sides of the angle. So, *P* is equidistant from lines *AC* and *AB*, and from lines *AB* and *BC*. By the transitive property, *P* is therefore equidistant from lines *AC* and *BC*. Thus, *P* is on the bisector of ∠*C*, and the three bisectors are concurrent at *P.*

ENRICHMENT 7–7

1. TASK, RATIO   2. FIFTH, TENTH   3. TRUE
4. FALSE   5. SIDE   6. TWO   7. OAT
8. MOM   9. ABOUT

The answer to the puzzle is:

"that it doesn't make four
But I fear that is almost too few."

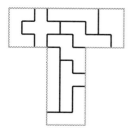

3.

4.

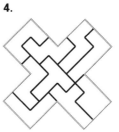

5.

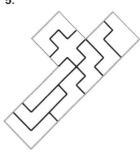

6.

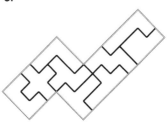

ENRICHMENT 7–8

1.

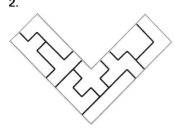

2.

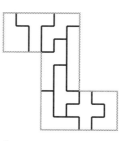

7.

8.

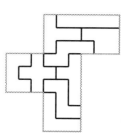

9.

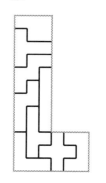

10.

11.

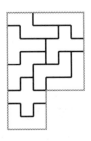

COMPUTER 7–5

1. $A2 = 6$, $C2 = 10$
2. $B2 = 4.5$, $C2 = 6$
3. Q, X; $A2/A1 = C2/C1$; $A2/A1 = B2/B1$
4. It will use Q if $A2 = 0$ and $B2 = 0$; it will use X if $A2 = 0$ and $C2 = 0$.
5. Nothing, the program stops.
6. Program is the same through line 60
   ```
   70  LET X = (B2*A1)/B1
   80  LET Y = (A2*B1)/A1
   90  LET Z = (B2*C1)/B1
   100 IF A2 = 0 THEN PRINT "A2="; X
   110 IF B2 = 0 THEN PRINT "B2 ="; Y
   120 IF C2 = 0 THEN PRINT "C2 = "; Z
   130 END
   ```

CALCULATOR 7–7

1. 34.0   2. 28.5   3. 245.9   4. 3,746.7
5. yes   6. no   7. yes   8. yes

Change lines 3 and 5. $:A/(.5(1 + \sqrt{5})) \to B$
:Disp "ENTER LENGTH OF LONG SIDE"

ENRICHMENT 8–1

Check students' tessellations for Exercises 1–7.

ENRICHMENT 8–2

1. order 8   2. order 3   3. order 9   4. order 3
5. order 5   6. order 8   7. order 4
8. order 6   9. order 6   10. $AO = 360°$
Answers will vary for Exercises 11–13.

ENRICHMENT 8–3

1. 1 side and 1 edge
2. 1 band, twice as long, half as wide, 4 half-twists
3. 2 bands, interlaced; 1 band like the original, 1 band twice as long and twice twisted
4. 2 bands, same length, half as wide, 2 half-twists
5. 1 band, twice as long, half as wide, 8 half-twists
6. 2 bands, each identical with the original except for being half as wide
7. 1 band with $2n + 2$ half-twists. n is the number of half-twists in the original band.

ENRICHMENT 8–4

2. 8 cm^3
3. 16 cm^3
4. ≈ 2.52 cm
5. $x = \sqrt[3]{2a^3}$ or $x = a\sqrt[3]{2}$

ENRICHMENT 8–5

Check students' tessellations for Exercises 1–4.

ENRICHMENT 8–6

1.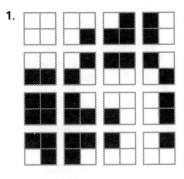

2. $\begin{bmatrix} 0 & 1 & 7 & 10 \\ 3 & 6 & 13 & 11 \\ 14 & 8 & 5 & 15 \\ 9 & 2 & 4 & 12 \end{bmatrix}$ 3. $\begin{bmatrix} 0 & 4 & 9 & 7 \\ 3 & 2 & 5 & 14 \\ 15 & 11 & 6 & 8 \\ 12 & 13 & 10 & 1 \end{bmatrix}$

4. *Answers will vary; sample answers given.*

$\begin{bmatrix} 0 & 4 & 8 & 5 \\ 3 & 2 & 1 & 6 \\ 15 & 11 & 7 & 10 \\ 12 & 13 & 14 & 9 \end{bmatrix}$ $\begin{bmatrix} 0 & 4 & 8 & 5 \\ 3 & 2 & 1 & 6 \\ 15 & 11 & 7 & 10 \\ 13 & 14 & 12 & 9 \end{bmatrix}$ $\begin{bmatrix} 0 & 4 & 12 & 9 \\ 3 & 2 & 1 & 7 \\ 15 & 10 & 5 & 14 \\ 13 & 11 & 6 & 8 \end{bmatrix}$

$\begin{bmatrix} 0 & 5 & 11 & 2 \\ 3 & 6 & 12 & 9 \\ 15 & 10 & 1 & 7 \\ 14 & 8 & 4 & 13 \end{bmatrix}$ $\begin{bmatrix} 0 & 5 & 11 & 3 \\ 2 & 4 & 13 & 15 \\ 10 & 1 & 7 & 14 \\ 9 & 6 & 12 & 8 \end{bmatrix}$ $\begin{bmatrix} 0 & 5 & 11 & 7 \\ 3 & 6 & 13 & 14 \\ 15 & 10 & 4 & 8 \\ 12 & 9 & 2 & 1 \end{bmatrix}$

$\begin{bmatrix} 0 & 5 & 14 & 8 \\ 2 & 4 & 9 & 3 \\ 10 & 1 & 7 & 15 \\ 11 & 6 & 12 & 13 \end{bmatrix}$ $\begin{bmatrix} 0 & 5 & 15 & 10 \\ 3 & 6 & 12 & 9 \\ 14 & 8 & 1 & 7 \\ 11 & 2 & 4 & 13 \end{bmatrix}$

ENRICHMENT 8–7

1. –1   2. 8   3. –3   4. 0   5. 0   6. 0
7. $3x + 4y + 5$ 8. $5y + 5$ 9. $-5x - 5$
10. $-a^2 - 3a + 6$ 11. $-a^2 - 7a - 6$ 12. $-a^2 + 5a + 6$

ENRICHMENT 8–8

1. $x = 2$, $y = 3$, $z = 5$
2. $x = 2$, $y = 3$, $z = -4$
3. $x = 0$, $y = 1$, $z = 2$
4. $x = 2.5$, $y = -1$, $z = -0.5$
5. Cramer's Rule cannot be used when the determinant of the coefficients equals 0.

ENRICHMENT 8–9

1. $\begin{bmatrix} 5 & -7 \\ -2 & 3 \end{bmatrix}$

2. $\begin{bmatrix} -5 & 7 \\ -2 & 3 \end{bmatrix}$

3. $\begin{bmatrix} -5 & -7 \\ 2 & 3 \end{bmatrix}$

4. $\begin{bmatrix} -5 & -7 \\ -2 & -3 \end{bmatrix}$

5. $\begin{bmatrix} 5 & 7 \\ 2 & 3 \end{bmatrix}$

6. $\begin{bmatrix} -\dfrac{5}{29} & \dfrac{7}{29} \\ \dfrac{2}{29} & \dfrac{3}{29} \end{bmatrix}$

7. $\begin{bmatrix} \dfrac{5}{29} & -\dfrac{7}{29} \\ \dfrac{2}{29} & \dfrac{3}{29} \end{bmatrix}$

8. $\begin{bmatrix} \dfrac{5}{29} & \dfrac{7}{29} \\ -\dfrac{2}{29} & \dfrac{3}{29} \end{bmatrix}$

9. $\begin{bmatrix} \dfrac{5}{29} & \dfrac{7}{29} \\ \dfrac{2}{29} & -\dfrac{3}{29} \end{bmatrix}$

10. When its determinant equals 0

COMPUTER 8–6

1. The three rows are: 33, 25, 27; 33, 48, 30; 29, 23, 34
2. Lines 70–130
3. Line 100
4. Each row of matrix A is entered one row at a time; then each row of matrix B is entered one row at a time.
5. TAB (75*J)/5
6. 10 DIM A(2, 3), B(2, 3)
   20 FOR I = 1 TO 2
   30 FOR J = 1 TO 3
   40   READ A(I, J)
   50 NEXT J
   60 NEXT I
   70 FOR I = 1 TO 2
   80   FOR J = 1 TO 3
   90   READ B(I, J)
   100   PRINT A(I, J) + B(I, J); TAB(75 * J / 3);
   110   NEXT J
   120   PRINT
   130 NEXT I
   140 PRINT
   150 DATA 6,2,3,4,–1,–5,10,–6,4,3,2,7
   160 END
   Result: row 1: 16, –4, 7; row 2: 7, 1, 2
7. row 1: –6, 0, 2; row 2: –8, –10, –4
8. Change 10 to DIM A(3,3)
   Change 20 to FOR I = 1 TO 3
   Change 50 to PRINT A(I,J) * 4; TAB(75 * J) / 3
   Change 100 to 8, 3, –2, 7, 0, 3, –5, 3, 9

CALCULATOR 8–8

1. Change the 2s in matrix [A] to 3s

2. $\begin{bmatrix} 3 & 9 & 24 & 18 \\ 3 & 12 & 12 & 3 \end{bmatrix}$

3. $\begin{bmatrix} -2 & -1 & 3 \\ -1 & -3 & -1 \end{bmatrix}$
   reflection over the *x*-axis

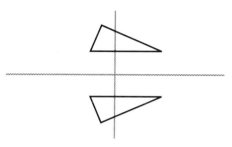

4. $\begin{bmatrix} 1 & 4 & 4 \\ 1 & 1 & -3 \end{bmatrix}$
   90° clockwise rotation

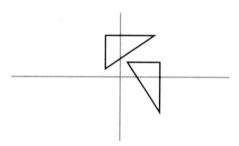

5. $\begin{bmatrix} -1 & -3 & -4 & -3 \\ 1 & 3 & 0 & -2 \end{bmatrix}$
   reflection over the line *y* = *x*

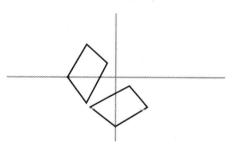

6. $\begin{bmatrix} -6 & -6 & 6 & 6 \\ -6 & 6 & 6 & -6 \end{bmatrix}$
   dilation, scale factor 3

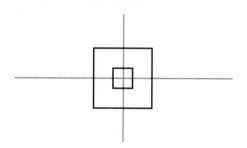

7. $\begin{bmatrix} 2 & 2 & 0 & -2 \\ 1 & -1 & -3 & -3 \end{bmatrix}$

rotation of 180°

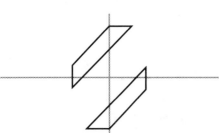

ENRICHMENT 9–1

1.

Sarah's Budget

Item	Amount Spent	Relative Spending	Degrees
Telephone	$26	13%	47°
Movies	$46	23%	83°
Books	$24	12%	43°
Car	$38	19%	68°
Other	$66	33%	119°

Sarah's Budget

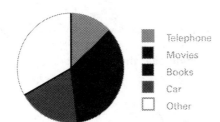

Telephone
Movies
Books
Car
Other

2.

Frank's Budget

Item	Amount Spent	Relative Spending	Degrees
Insurance	$800	16%	58°
Car	$1,600	32%	115°
Mortgage	$1,800	36%	130°
Utilities	$600	12%	43°
Other	$200	4%	14°

Frank's Budget

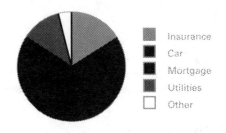

Insurance
Car
Mortgage
Utilities
Other

ENRICHMENT 9–2

1.

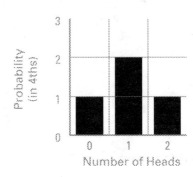

2.

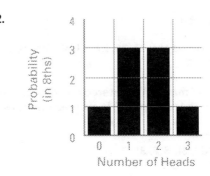

3.

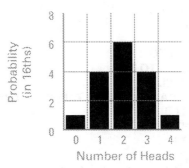

4.

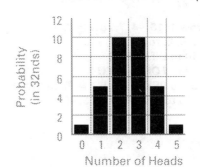

5.

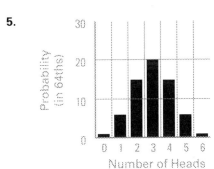

6.

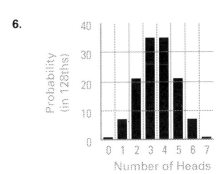

7.

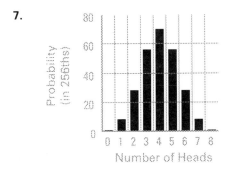

8.

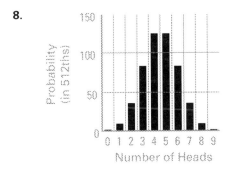

9.

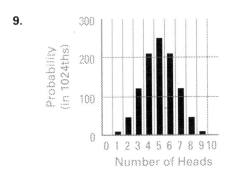

10. Histogram approaches the bell or normal curve.

ENRICHMENT 9–3

All the numbers in the grid are perfect squares. Four of them (1, 64, 729, and 4096) are also perfect sixth powers and thus perfect cubes. The probability of getting 2 of these 4 numbers is:

$$\frac{_4C_2}{_{64}C_2} = \frac{1}{336}$$

ENRICHMENT 9–4

1.

$$
\begin{array}{ccc}
X_4 & X_2 & O_1 \\
X_5 & O_3 & O_2 \\
O_4 & X_3 & X_1
\end{array}
\qquad
\begin{array}{ccc}
O_4 & X_5 & X_4 \\
X_3 & O_3 & X_2 \\
X_1 & O_2 & O_1
\end{array}
$$

$$
\begin{array}{ccc}
X_1 & O_2 & O_1 \\
X_3 & O_3 & X_2 \\
O_4 & X_5 & X_4
\end{array}
\qquad
\begin{array}{ccc}
O_4 & X_3 & X_1 \\
X_5 & O_3 & O_2 \\
X_4 & X_2 & O_1
\end{array}
$$

$$
\begin{array}{ccc}
X_1 & X_3 & O_4 \\
O_2 & O_3 & X_5 \\
O_1 & X_2 & X_4
\end{array}
\qquad
\begin{array}{ccc}
X_4 & X_5 & O_4 \\
X_2 & O_3 & X_3 \\
O_1 & O_2 & X_1
\end{array}
$$

$$
\begin{array}{ccc}
O_1 & X_2 & X_4 \\
O_2 & O_3 & X_5 \\
X_1 & X_3 & O_4
\end{array}
$$

2.

$$
\begin{array}{ccc}
O_1 & X_1 & O_2 \\
X_2 & O_3 & X_3 \\
X_4 & X_5 & O_4
\end{array}
\qquad
\begin{array}{ccc}
X_4 & X_2 & O_1 \\
X_5 & O_3 & X_1 \\
O_4 & X_3 & O_2
\end{array}
$$

$$
\begin{array}{ccc}
O_4 & X_5 & X_4 \\
X_3 & O_3 & X_2 \\
O_2 & X_1 & O_1
\end{array}
\qquad
\begin{array}{ccc}
O_2 & X_3 & O_4 \\
X_1 & O_3 & X_5 \\
O_1 & X_2 & X_4
\end{array}
$$

3. 62
4. 16
5. 9! ÷ 5!4! = 126
6. 16 ÷ 126 ≈ 0.127

Note: There are 36 other arrangements in which either A or B can win. In these, A's chances are 13/40; B's chances are 27/40.

ENRICHMENT 9–5

1.

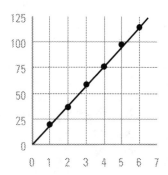

2. Pascal's Triangle. Each number equals the sum of the two above it.

3. $_nC_r + {}_nC_{r+1} = {}_{n+1}C_{r+1}$

ENRICHMENT 9–6

1. Equation: $y = 19.3x - 0.6$
   $r = 0.9994$

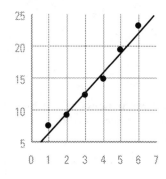

2. Equation: $y = 3.2x - 3.2$
   $r = 0.9899$

3. Equation: $y = 2.6x + 55.6$
   $r = 0.9581$

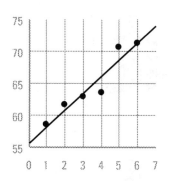

ENRICHMENT 9–7

1. 3, 6, 6, 8 minutes

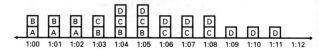

2. 3, 5, 8, 8 minutes

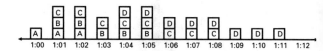

ENRICHMENT 9–8

1. $A_s = \dfrac{45 + 60}{2}$
   $A_s = 52.5$ mi/h

2. $A_s = \dfrac{2}{\frac{1}{40} + \frac{1}{25}}$
   $A_s = 30.769$ mi/h

3. $A_s = \dfrac{2}{\frac{1}{25} + \frac{1}{18}}$
   $A_s = 20.93$ mi/h

4. $A_s = \dfrac{62 + 58}{2}$
   $A_s = 60$ mi/h

5. $A_s = \dfrac{4}{\frac{1}{120.8} + \frac{1}{132.3} + \frac{1}{141.6} + \frac{1}{127.3}}$
   $A_s = 130.06$ mi/h

CALCULATOR 9–2

Answers will vary for Exercises 1–7.
Sample answers are given for Exercises 6–7.

6. Prgm #: SPINNER
   : ClrHome
   : Disp "SPIN"
   : Pause
   : Int 8Rand + 1 → S
   : Disp S
   : Stop

7. Prgm #: COINTOSS

```
: ClrHome
: Disp "TOSS TWO COINS"
: Pause
: Int 2Rand + 1 → A
: Int 2Rand + 1 → B
: If A = 1
: Disp "H"
: If A = 2
: Disp "T"
: If B = 1
: Disp "H"
: If B = 2
: Disp "T"
: Stop
```

COMPUTER 9–5

1. 60,480
2. 181,440
3. 362,880
4. 720
5. 5,040
6. 30,240
7. $\leq$
8. The program goes to Line 200, with $C = N$; lines 210 to 230 compute $N!$. Then program returns to line 50 and assigns $N!$ to the variable X.
9. $(N - R)!$
10. *Answers will vary.*
11. *Answers will vary. Possible answer:*
    205 IF C = 0 THEN 240
12. 40,320
13. 40,320
14. 5040
15. 5040
16. 362,880
17. 362,880
18. The result is always $N!$, or $_NP_N = {}_NP_{N-1}$
19. INPUT N, R
    GOSUB 200
    LET C = R
    GOSUB 200
    X / (Y * Z)
20. 28
21. 210
22. 792
23. 28
24. 210
25. 792
26. $_NC_R$

ENRICHMENT 10–1

1. triangle: 0.4; pentagon: 1.7; hexagon: 2.6; octagon: 4.8
2. triangle: 1.7; pentagon: 6.9; hexagon: 10.4; octagon: 19.3
3. triangle: 3.9; pentagon: 15.5; hexagon: 23.4; octagon: 43.5
4. 5.4 sq cm
5. 5.7 sq cm
6. 5.0 sq cm
7. 6.2 sq cm
8. 6.2 sq cm
9. 7.4 sq cm

ENRICHMENT 10–2

1. $B^2 + C^2 - 2cx$
2. $b^2 + c^2 + 2cx$

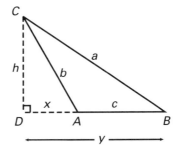

3. 3.9 + 6.9 = 10.8
4. 4.5 + 8 = 12.5

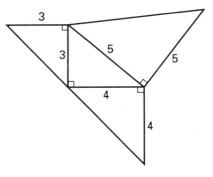

5. 3.5 + 6.3 = 9.8

ENRICHMENT 10–3

1.

2.

3.

4.

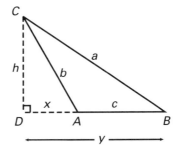

5.

6.

7.

8.

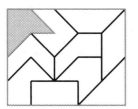

9.

10.

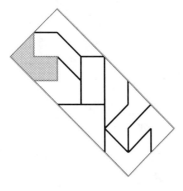

1.

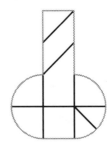

2.

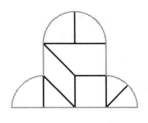

3.

4.

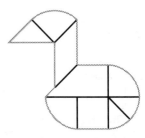

5.

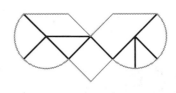

6.

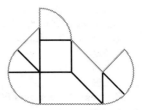

7.

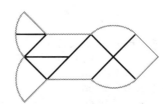

8.

9.

10. *Answers will vary. You may wish to have pairs of students exchange and solve puzzles.*

ENRICHMENT (vertical sidebar)

1.

2. There are 9 in all.

3. There are 20 in all.

 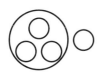

ENRICHMENT 10–6

1. 5. right; semicircle

6. *XCD*

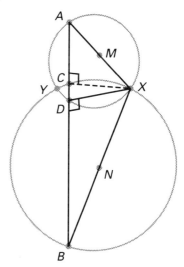

2.

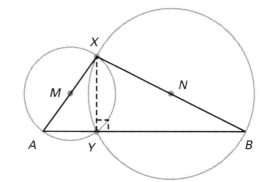

3. When you draw segment *AB*, it passes through the point *Y*. This point is on both circles. So, points *C* and *D* do not exist. And, △*XDC* doesn't exist either.

ENRICHMENT 10–7

Check students' constructions for Exercises 1–8.

ENRICHMENT 10–8

Check students' constructions for Exercises 1–8.

COMPUTER 10–1

1. irrational   2. rational
3. irrational   4. rational
5. Line 40 IF X^(1/2) – INT(X ^ (1/2)) = 0 THEN 70
6. 10 PRINT "IS THE CUBE ROOT OF YOUR NUMBER
     RATIONAL?"
     20 PRINT "ENTER YOUR NUMBER." 30 INPUT X
     40 IF X^ (1/3) – INT(X^ (1/3)) = 0 THEN 70
     50 PRINT "CUBE ROOT OF"; X; "IS IRRATIONAL."
     60 END
     70 PRINT "CUBE ROOT OF"; X; "IS RATIONAL."
7. rational   8. rational
9. irrational   10. rational
11. 2   12. 3   13. 10   14. 4   15. 7   16. 8

CALCULATOR 10–2

1. y greater than or equal to x, x or y less than zero
2. $x = 4$, $y = 2$ or $x = 5$, $y = 3$

ENRICHMENT 11–1

1. 10_{ten} 2. 15_{ten} 3. 26_{ten} 4. 1.5_{ten}
5. 0.25_{ten} 6. 2.75_{ten} 7. 1001_{two} 8. 10100_{two}
9. 11111_{two} 10. 1.11_{two} 11. 10.01_{two}
12. 0.101_{two}

ENRICHMENT 11–2

1.

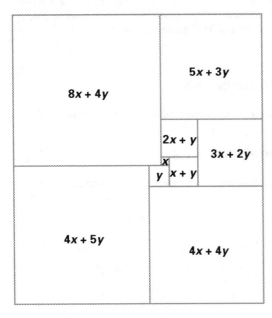

2.

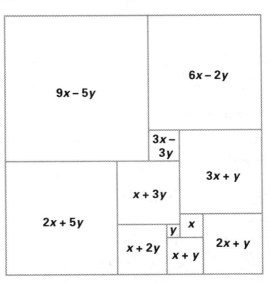

3. The left and right sides must be equal, so
$5x + 2y = x + 2y$. Solving for x gives $x = 0$. So, the
center square is really a point; the large rectangle
is really a square divided in four quarters. Thus, it
is not a squared rectangle.

ENRICHMENT 11–3

1. 17   2. 41   3. 31   4. 23   5. 12   6. 1
7. 53   8. 43   9. 67   10. 3   11. 7   12. 72

ENRICHMENT 11–4

1. $S = \dfrac{100(1 + 100)}{2} = 5{,}050$

2. $S = \dfrac{101(0 + 100)}{2} = 5{,}050$

3. $S = \dfrac{8(3 + 24)}{2} = 108$

4. $S = \dfrac{9(10 + 50)}{2} = 270$

5. $S = \dfrac{50(2 + 100)}{2} = 2{,}550$

6. $S = \dfrac{n(2 + n)}{4}$

7. $S = \dfrac{50(1 + 99)}{2} = 2{,}500$

8. $S = \dfrac{(1 + n)^2}{4}$

9. $S = \dfrac{21(-10 + 10)}{2} = 0$

10. $S = \dfrac{(2x + 1)(-x + x)}{2} = 0$

ENRICHMENT

ENRICHMENT 11–5

1. $XY(x - y)$
2. $XY(x + y)$
3. $Y^2(x - y)$
4. $2y^3 + y^2(x - y) + xy(x - y)$
5. $x^2(x - y) + y^3 + x^2y$
6. $x^2y + y^3 + y^2(x - y) + xy(x + y)$

Answers will vary for Exercises 7–9.

ENRICHMENT 11–6

1.	1, 2, 7	10	Deficient
2.	1, 2, 3	6	Perfect
3.	1, 2, 3, 4, 6	16	Abundant
4.	1, 2, 4, 5, 10	22	Abundant
5.	1, 2, 3, 5, 6, 10, 15	42	Abundant
6.	1, 2, 4, 7, 8, 14, 28	64	Abundant
7.	1	1	Deficient
8.	1, 2, 4, 37, 74	118	Deficient
9.	1, 2, 4, 53, 106	166	Deficient
10.	1, 2, 4, 8, 16, 31, 62, 124, 248	496	Perfect
11.	1, 7, 143	151	Deficient

12. 6; 28; 496; 8,128; 33,550,336; 8,589,869,056; 137,438,691,328

ENRICHMENT 11–7

1.

2.

3.

4.

ENRICHMENT 11–8

1. $(a^2 + a + 1)(a^2 - a + 1)$
2. $(a^2 + a - 1)(a^2 - a - 1)$
3. $(2a^2 + a + 2)(2a^2 - a + 2)$
4. $(2a^2 + a - 2)(2a^2 - a - 2)$
5. $(3a^2 + 3a + 1)(3a^2 - 3a + 1)$
6. $(3a^2 + 3a - 1)(3a^2 - 3a - 1)$
7. $(2a^2 + 3a + 1)(2a^2 - 3a + 1)$
8. $(2a^2 + 3a - 1)(2a^2 - 3a - 1)$

ENRICHMENT 11–9

1. $(a - b)(a^2 + ab + b^2)$
2. $(a - b)(a^4 + a^3b + a^2b^2 + ab^3 + b^4)$
3. $(a - b)(a^6 + a^5b + a^4b^2 + a^3b^3 + a^2b^4 + ab^5 + b^6)$
4. $(a - b)(a^8 + a^7b + a^6b^2 + a^5b^3 + a^4b^4 + a^3b^5 + a^2b^6 + ab^7 + b^8)$
5. $(a + b)(a^2 - ab + b^2)$
6. $(a + b)(a^4 - a^3b + a^2b^2 - ab^3 + b^4)$
7. $(a + b)(a^6 - a^5b + a^4b^2 - a^3b^3 + a^2b^4 - ab^5 + b^6)$
8. $(a + b)(a^8 - a^7b + a^6b^2 - a^5b^3 + a^4b^4 - a^3b^5 + a^2b^6 - ab^7 + b^8)$

ENRICHMENT 11–10

$2 = (4 - 3) + (2 - 1)$
$3 = (4 - 3) + (2 \times 1)$
$4 = (4 - 2) + (3 - 1)$
$5 = (4 - 2) + (3 \times 1)$
$6 = 4 + 3 + 1 - 2$
$7 = 3(4 - 1) - 2$
$8 = 4 + 3 + 2 - 1$
$9 = 4 + 2 + (3 \times 1)$
$10 = 4 + 3 + 2 + 1$
$11 = (4 \times 3) - (2 - 1)$
$12 = (4 \times 3) \times (2 - 1)$
$13 = (4 \times 3) + (2 - 1)$
$14 = (4 \times 3) + (2 \times 1)$
$16 = (4 \times 2) \times (3 - 1)$
$17 = 3(4 + 2) - 1$
$18 = (2 \times 3) \times (4 - 1)$
$20 = 21 - (4 - 3)$
$21 = (4 + 3) \times (2 + 1)$
$22 = 21 + (4 - 3)$
$24 = (4 + 2) \times (3 + 1)$
$25 = (2 + 3) \times (4 + 1)$
$26 = 24 + (3 - 1)$
$27 = 3^2 \times (4 - 1)$
$28 = 21 + 4 + 3$
$30 = (2 \times 3) \times (4 + 1)$
$31 = 34 - (2 + 1)$
$32 = 4^2 \times (3 - 1)$
$33 = 21 + (4 \times 3)$
$34 = 2 \times (14 + 3)$

$36 = 34 + (2 \times 1)$
$37 = 31 + 4 + 2$
$38 = 42 - (1 + 3)$
$39 = 42 - (1 \times 3)$
$40 = 41 - (3 - 2)$
$41 = 43 - (2 \times 1)$
$42 = 43 - (2 - 1)$
$44 = 43 + (2 - 1)$
$45 = 43 + (2 \times 1)$
$46 = 43 + (2 + 1)$
$47 = 31 + 4^2$
$48 = 4^2 \times (3 \times 1)$
$49 = 41 + 2^3$
$50 = 41 + 3^2$

Other answers are possible.

CALCULATOR 11–8

1. $(x - 7)(x - 2)$

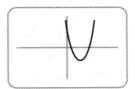

2. $(x + 4)(x - 1)$

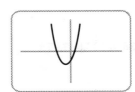

3. $(x - 2)(x - 4)$

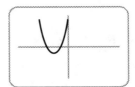

4. $(x - 6)(x + 2)$

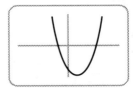

5. $(x + 2)(x + 1)$

6. $(x - 3)(x - 2)$

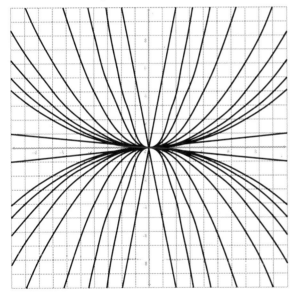

COMPUTER 11–10

1. $(3x + 5)(x + 2)$
2. $(2x + 1)(x + 2)$
3. $(3x + 4)(2x + 3)$
4. $(2x + 3)(x + 5)$
5. factors of A
6. factors of C
7. The program goes on to find factors for C and to test combinations of those factors with the factors of A to check that the sum of the outer and inner products is B.
8. The program stops and prints out as soon as it finds a combination that works.

ENRICHMENT 12–1

Answers will vary.

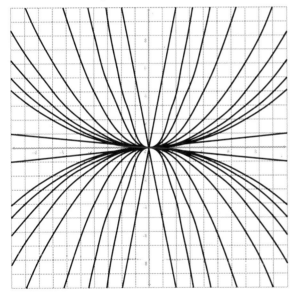

ENRICHMENT 12–2

1. 1, 5, 12, 22, 35
   $1.5n^2 - 0.5n$
2. 1, 6, 15, 28, 45
   $2n^2 - n$
3. 1, 8, 21, 40, 65
   $3n^2 - 2n$

ENRICHMENT 12–3

1. $y = -\frac{1}{8}x^2 - \frac{1}{2}x + 4$

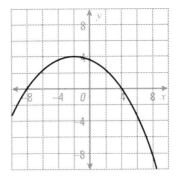

2. $y = -\frac{1}{4}x^2 - \frac{1}{4}x + 1$

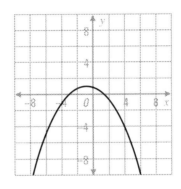

3. $y = \frac{1}{15}x^2 + \frac{7}{15}x - 2$

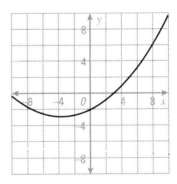

4. *Answers will vary.*

ENRICHMENT 12–4

1. $x = 3$, $x = -1$
   $y = -(x - 3)^2(x + 1)$

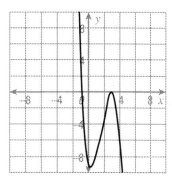

2. $x = 3$, $x = -1$
   $y = (x - 3)^2(x + 1)$

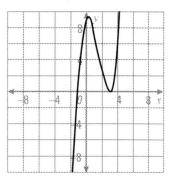

3. $x = 6$, $x = 5$, $x = 2$
   $y = -(x - 6)(x - 5)(x - 2)$

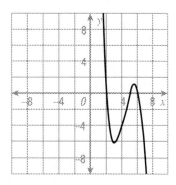

4. $x = -5$, $x = -2$, $x = -1$
   $y = (x + 5)(x + 2)(x + 1)$

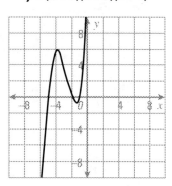

5. $x = -4$, $x = 2$, $x = -1$
   $y = -(x + 4)(x - 2)(x + 1)$

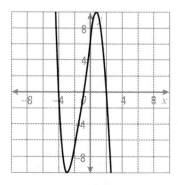

6. $x = 4$, $x = -2$, $x = 1$
   $y = -(x - 4)(x + 2)(x - 1)$

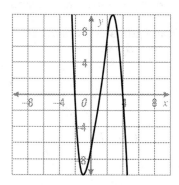

ENRICHMENT 12–5

5	80	59	73	61	3	63	12	13
1	2	5	3	5	2	7	2	81
4	1	3	5	2	6	3	6	78
76	5	4	3	4	4	3	2	6
7	6	3	4	4	3	4	1	75
74	6	4	4	3	4	3	1	8
67	1	4	3	5	2	5	7	15
66	5	2	5	2	5	1	6	16
69	2	23	9	21	79	19	70	77

ENRICHMENT 12–6

1.

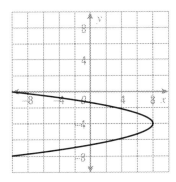

2.

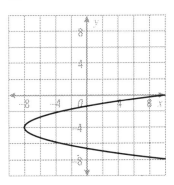

3.

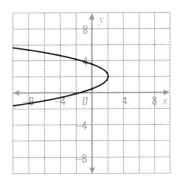

4.

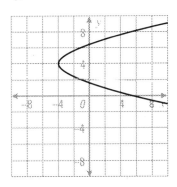

5.

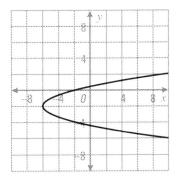

6.

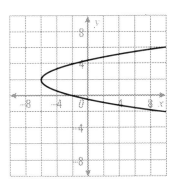

ENRICHMENT 12–7

1. 4.36
2. 3
3. 9.95
4. 4.58 and 3.74 units
5. sides: 7, 7, 9.9; area: 24.5
6. $z = \dfrac{x^2}{2ca^2}$ $z = \dfrac{y^2}{2ca^2}$

ENRICHMENT 12–8

1. 43   2. 47   3. 53   4. 61   5. 71   6. 83
7. 97   8. 113   9. 131   10. 151   11. 173
12. 197   13. 223   14. 251   15. 281   16. 313
17. 347   18. 383   19. 421   20. 461
21. All of them are prime.
22. When solved, $(4p - 163)$ is under a radial.
    $(4p - 163)$ must be greater than 0, so $p > 40.75$.
23. No. Primes omitted between 40 and 462 are 59,
    67, 73, 79, 89, 101, 103, 107, 109, and others.
24. $x = 40$ gives 1,681, which is 41^2

CALCULATOR 12–6

1. 169   2   2. 0   1
3. 0   1   4. −23   0
5. 48   2   6. −47   0
7. two   8. one   9. zero   10. 1; −3, −4
11. 0; 1   12. −12; No real solutions
13. 16; 3, −1   14. −7; No real solutions
15. 225; 2.5, −5

COMPUTER 12–7

1. yes
2. no
3. 60 LET BC = SQR((X2 – X3) ^ 2 + (Y2 – Y3) ^ 2)
   70 LET DA = SQR((X4 – X1) ^ 2 + (Y4 – Y1) ^ 2)
   80 IF AB = CD AND BC = DA THEN 110
   90 PRINT "QUADRILATERAL IS NOT A
        PARALLELOGRAM."
   100 END
   110 PRINT "ABCD IS A PARALLELOGRAM."
4. yes
5. no
6. 80 IF AB = BC AND BC = CD AND CD = DA THEN
        110
   90 PRINT "QUADRILATERAL IS NOT A
        RHOMBUS."
   100 END
   110 PRINT "QUADRILATERAL IS A RHOMBUS."
7. yes
8. no
9. LET SAB = (Y2 – Y1)/(X2–X1)
10. IF SAB = –(1/SBC) THEN PRINT "AB IS
    PERPENDICULAR TO BC."
11. yes
12. no
13. parallel to the x-axis.
14. If X2 – X3 = 0, then the line segments are
    perpendicular.

ENRICHMENT 13–1

1.

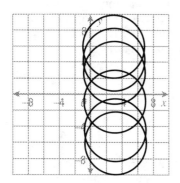

2.

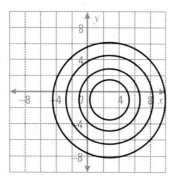

3.

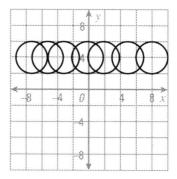

4.

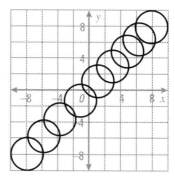

5.

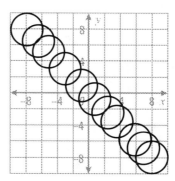

6.

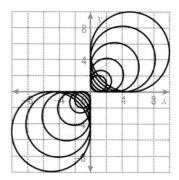

ENRICHMENT 13–2

1. $y = x^2$
   $y = 0.67x^2$
   $y = 0.5x^2$
   $y = 0.4x^2$
   $y = 0.33x^2$
2. The greater the distance, the wider the opening.
3. F is the focus and the line through $\overline{EC}$ is the directrix. As the pencil moves, $\overline{FP}$ is always equal to $\overline{CP}$. This is the definition of the parabola.

ENRICHMENT 13–3

1.
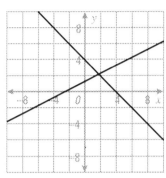

2.
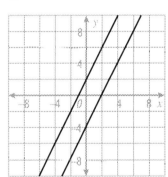

3.
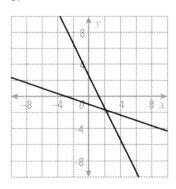

4.
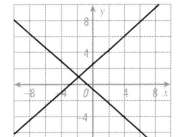

ENRICHMENT 13–4

Answers will vary for Exercises 1–2.
3. $m = -0.5$ 4. $m = 3$

5. $m = 0.4$ 6. $m = -\dfrac{x_1}{y_1}$

ENRICHMENT 13–5

Check students' work for Exercises 1–4.
5. an ellipse

ENRICHMENT 13–6

1. 31524–15243–12453–24531–23451–12345
2. 32415–34125–53412–25341–23451–12345 or
   32415–34125–53412–51342–13425–12345
3. Many solutions are correct. There are 60 (out of 120 in all) possible such arrangements.

ENRICHMENT 13–7

1. B   2. C   3. D   4. A

ENRICHMENT 13–8

1.
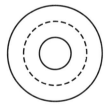

2.

3.

4.

5.

6.

7. a tilted ellipse with center at O

CALCULATOR 13–3

1.

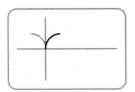

2.

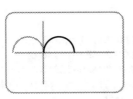

3.

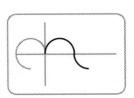

4.

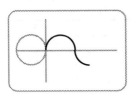

5.

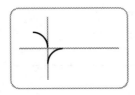

6.

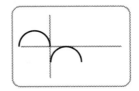

7.

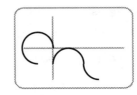

8.

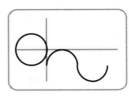

9.

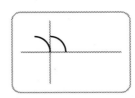

10.

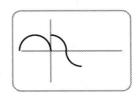

11.

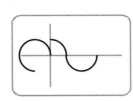

12.

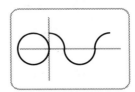

ENRICHMENT

13.

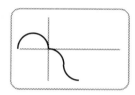

14.

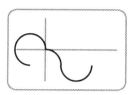

15.

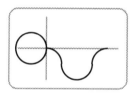

16.

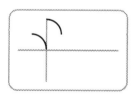

17.

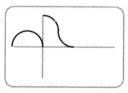

18.

19.

20.

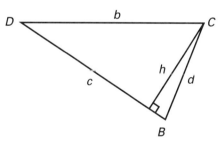

COMPUTER 13–4

1. Subtract x^2 from 25; result is y^2
2. It takes the square root of the value found for y^2.
4. Only half of the circle is graphed. In Column C, only positive square roots are printed. Have Column D print $(-1)Y$ for the negative square root of Y.
5. B3: +16 – A3^2
6. D3: +(–1)*C3
7. B3: +(16–X^2)/4
8. Ellipse; $9x^2 + y^2 = 36$

ENRICHMENT 14–1

1. hypotenuse	2. y-axis
3. tables	4. height
5. right	6. area
7. tangent	8. cosine
9. opposite	10. ratios
11. degree	12. sine
13. adjacent	14. trigonometric

Answer to the puzzle is "Pythagorean Theorem."

ENRICHMENT 14–2

1. $A = 0.5\,ch$; $\sin B = h/d$;
   $h = d \sin B$; $A = 0.5\,cd \sin B$

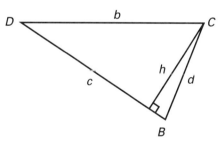

2. 1,532.1 sq units
3. 283.4 sq units
4. 225.7 sq units
5. 119.7 sq units

ENRICHMENT 14–3

1. 0° or 360°   2. 180°   3. 90°   4. 225°   5. 45°
6. 135°   7. 292.5°   8. 22.5°   9. 202.5°
10. 119.3 mph, 123°   11. 144.3 mph, 256°
12. 98.6 mph, 60°   13. 100 mph, 37°
14. 148.4 mph, 123°   15. 109.7 mph, 336°

ENRICHMENT 14–4

1. $\frac{\pi}{6}$ 2. $\frac{-2\pi}{3}$ 3. $\frac{3\pi}{2}$ 4. $\frac{\pi}{8}$ 5. 90°

6. –450°   7. 540°   8. 135°

9.

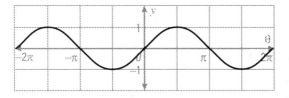

10.

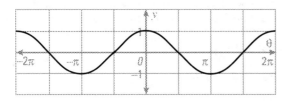

ENRICHMENT 14–5

1.

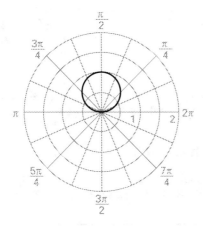

2.

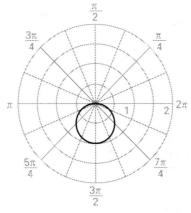

3.

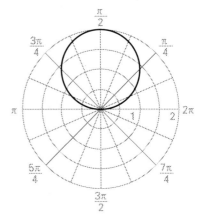

4.

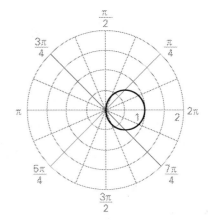

5.

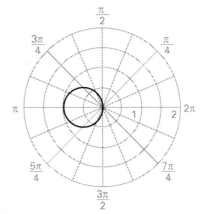

6.

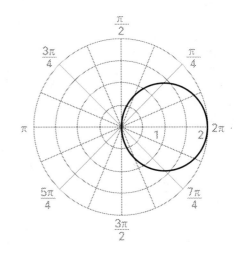

1.

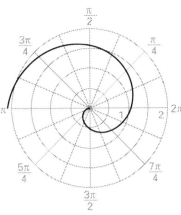

2.

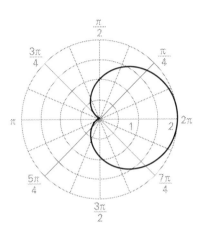

3.

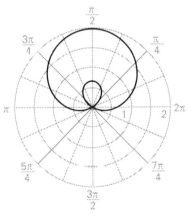

4.

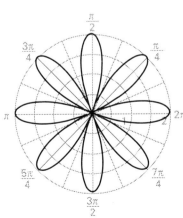

5.

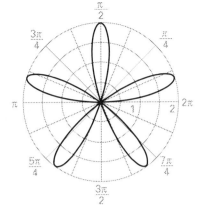

6.

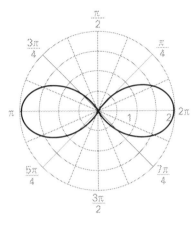

7.

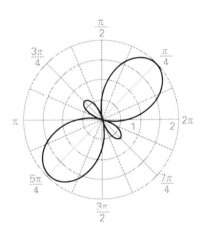

8.

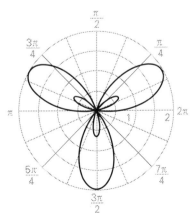

9.

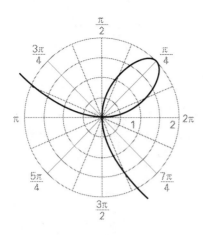

COMPUTER 14–2

1.	30	**60**	5	**3**	**6**
2.	50	**40**	**5**	6	**8**
3.	45	**45**	**7**	**7**	10
4.	25	**65**	**17**	8	**19**

5. 80 PRINT "A = "; C * SIN(R); ", B = "; C * COS(R)
6. $r = \pi d/180$

CALCULATOR 14–5

5. The *y*-value of the sum of the curves is the sum of the *y*-values of the two curves.
   $Y_3 = Y_1 + Y_2$

ENRICHMENT

ACHIEVEMENT 1A

1. {5, 7, 9, 11 . . .}
2. {a}, {b}, {a, b}, ∅
3. −8
4. −8
5. −1.6, −$\frac{1}{2}$, $\sqrt{3}$, $2\frac{2}{5}$, **left to right as marked**

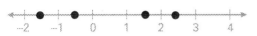

6.

7. −3
8. 3
9. −3
10. {1, 2, 3, 5, 9}
11. { }
12. Graph of *A*:

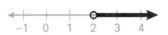

Graph of *B*:

Graph of *A* ∩ *B*:

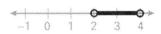

Solution Set: {*x*|*x* is a real number and 2 < *x* < 4}

13. Graph of *A*:

Graph of *B*:

Graph of *A* ∪ *B*:

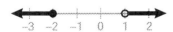

Solution Set: {*x*|*x* is a real number and *x* > 1 or *x* ≤ −2}

14. 2.42   15. 2.08   16. $3\frac{11}{12}$ 17. $-2\frac{4}{6}$ or $-2\frac{2}{3}$
18. −3.38   19. −0.6   20. $-1\frac{1}{8}$ 21. $1\frac{3}{4}$
22. −0.1   23. 0.3   24. −0.1   25. −0.3
26. 0.12   27. 1.2   28. 3   29. 12   30. 4
31. −27   32. 18   33. −12   34. −0.9   35. 2
36. x^8 37. y^6 38. a^4b^4 39. a^3 40. m^{-6}

41. a^{-8} 42. k^{13} 43. n^{-14} 44. $\frac{1}{16}$ 45. $\frac{1}{8}$
46. $\frac{1}{8}$ 47. $3\frac{15}{16}$ 48. 1.293×10^8
49. 6.5×10^{-3} 50. 42,000   51. 0.0213
52. $18/g   53. 151

ACHIEVEMENT 1B

1. {4, 2, 0, −2 . . .}
2. {m}, {n}, {m,n}, ∅
3. −4
4. 16
5. $-1\frac{1}{2}$, $\sqrt{2}$, $3\frac{1}{12}$, 4.5, **left to right as marked**

6.

7. 4
8. 4
9. −4
10. {3}
11. {1, 2, 3, 6, 8}
12. Graph of *A*:

Graph of *B*:

Graph of *A* ∩ *B*:

Solution Set: {*x*|*x* is a real number and −1 < *x* ≤ 2}

13. Graph of *A*:

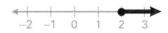

Graph of *B*:

Graph of *A* ∪ *B*:

Solution Set: {*x*|*x* is a real number and *x* ≥ 2 or *x* < −1}

14. −2.38   15. 3.49   16. $-2\frac{13}{24}$ 17. $\frac{5}{12}$

18. 4.86   19. −1.2   20. $-\frac{5}{6}$ 21. −2

22. −1.1   23. 2.1   24. −1.1   25. −2.1   26. 8
27. 16   28. 32   29. 0.08   30. 4   31. 27
32. −18   33. 12   34. 0.5   35. 22   36. x^5
37. y^8 38. a^6b^6 39. a^{10} 40. m^{-16} 41. a^{-7}

42. k^{14} 43. n^3 44. $\frac{1}{9}$ 45. $\frac{1}{-64}$ or $-\frac{1}{64}$

46. $\frac{1}{16}$ 47. $15\frac{8}{9}$

48. 7.3×10^{-4} 49. 1.74532×10^9 50. 0.00821
51. 24,160   52. $2/g   53. 133

ACHIEVEMENT 2A

1. −4, −8, −12   2. 48, −96, 192
3. 16, 25, 36   4. 5, 0, −6
5. Function: No   6. Function: Yes
   Domain: {2, 3, 4}   Domain: {6, 7, 8, 9}
   Range: {3, 4}   Range: {3, 5, 9}
7. 5   8. 7   9. 23
10.

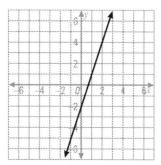

11. 14   12. 4   13. 19   14. $a = -11$
15. $b = -81$ 16. $c = 1$ 17. $d = -1$ 18. $e = 7$
19. $j = 16$ 20. $k = 5$ 21. $l = 20$ 22. $m = 3$
23. $q = -5$
24. $r \geq -2$

25. $s > -4$

26.

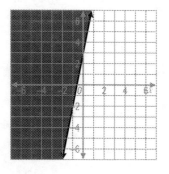

27.

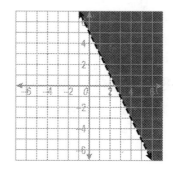

28.   Weekly Hours

Hrs	Tally	Freq
9	I	1
10		0
11	III	3
12	II	2
13	I	1
14		0
15	I	1
16	I	1
17		0
18		0
19		0
20	I	1

29. Mean: 13
    Median: 12
    Mode: 11

30.   Wage Increase

0	0	5		
1	0	5	2	5
2	5	0	0	
3				
4	0			

31. Outliers: 40
    Clusters: 5–25
    Gaps: 25–40

32.

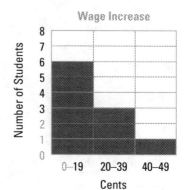

33. x = 4   34. x = 1   35. x = 3
36.

	A	B	C	D
1	30	120	**15**	**105**
2	**60**	**240**	**30**	**210**
3	**90**	**360**	**45**	**315**
4	**120**	**480**	**60**	**420**

ACHIEVEMENT 2B

1. 13, 16, 19
2. 81, –243, 729
3. 64, 125, 216
4. 15, 21, 28
5. Function: Yes
   Domain: {1, 2, 4, 5}
   Range: {1, 2, 5}
6. Function: No
   Domain: {1, 2, 3}
   Range: {5, 6, 7, 8}
7. –6   8. 12   9. 3
10.

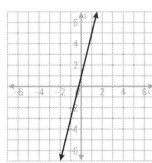

11. 5   12. 1   13. 1   14. a = 12   15. b = 64
16. c = 1   17. d = 38   18. e = 12   19. j = 36
20. k = 8   21. l = 63   22. m = 20   23. q = 0
24. r ≥ 5

25. s < 4

26.

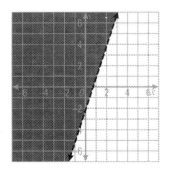

27.

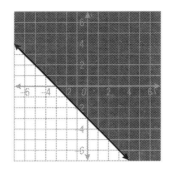

28.   Math Quiz Scores

Score	Tally	Freq
86	I	1
87	I	1
88		0
89	II	2
90		0
91	I	1
92		0
93	IIII	4
94		0
95		0
96	I	1

29. Mean: 91
Median: 92
Mode: 93

30.   Math Quiz Scores

4	8		
5			
6	1	5	
7	7	3	
8	3	7	8
9	3	6	

31. Outliers: 48
Clusters: 61–96
Gaps: 48–61

32.

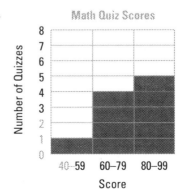

Math Quiz Scores

33. $x = -1$ **34.** $x = 5$ **35.** $x = -3$
36.

	A	B	C	D
1	150	30	180	36
2	125	25	150	30
3	100	20	120	24
4	75	15	90	18

ACHIEVEMENT 3A

1. 10   2. 8   3. 3   4. 10   5. 94   6. 34
7. $\angle UMX, \angle UMY, \angle VMY, \angle VMZ$
8. $\angle UMW, \angle VMX, \angle WMZ$
9. 55°
10. point G, –4
11. $\overline{LN}, \overline{KO}$
12. 26°   13. 116°   14. 52°
15. $\angle 2$ and $\angle 3$; $\angle 1$ and $\angle 4$; $\angle 5$ and $\angle 8$; $\angle 6$ and $\angle 7$
16. $\angle 3$ and $\angle 6$; $\angle 4$ and $\angle 5$
17. 90°   18. 40°   19. 90°   20. 140°   21. 50°
22. 130°
23. The thirtieth figure will be 30 rows of 30 dots, or 30^2 dots.
24. *Sample answer.*
    Converse: If all the vertical angles are equal, then two parallel lines are cut by a transversal. Original condition is true. Converse is false.
    Counterexample: Two intersecting lines.
25. *Check students' drawings.*
26. *Check students' drawings.*
27. Statements
    2. right
    3. 90°
    4. *AXB;* m$\angle 2$
    5. m$\angle 1$ + m$\angle 2$
    Reasons
    1. given
    2. perpendicular
    3. right angle
    4. angle addition
28. Andy, surgeon; Luisa, psychiatrist; Carl, counselor; Ann, nurse

ACHIEVEMENT 3B

1. 5   2. 3   3. 7   4. 2   5. 91   6. 33
7. $\angle OAP, \angle OAQ, \angle PAQ, \angle PAR, \angle QAS, \angle QAR,$ $\angle RAS, \angle RAT, \angle SAT$
8. $\angle OAT$
9. 66°
10. point G, 3
11. $\overline{AG}, \overline{BF}, \overline{CE}$
12. 45°   13. 90°   14. 180°
15. $\angle 1$ and $\angle 5$; $\angle 2$ and $\angle 6$; $\angle 3$ and $\angle 7$; $\angle 4$ and $\angle 8$

16. $\angle 1$ and $\angle 8$; $\angle 2$ and $\angle 7$
17. 60°   18. 150°   19. 180°   20. 150°   21. 60°
22. 30°
23. 120 squares
24. Converse: If vertical angles are equal, then two lines intersect. Original statement and converse are true.
25. *Check students' drawings.*
26. *Check students' drawings.*
27. Statements
    1. $\overrightarrow{XM}$ intersects *LN,* $\angle 1$ and $\angle 2$ are adjacent
    2. straight
    3. 180°
    4. *LXN;* m$\angle 2$
    5. $m\angle 1 + m\angle 2$
    Reasons
    1. given
    2. straight angle
    3. straight angle
    4. adjacent angles
28. Kirk, baseball; Alicia, tennis; Marsha, cheerleading; Chad, drama

ACHIEVEMENT 4A

1. 120
2. 68
3. Statements
    1. $\overline{QN} \cong \overline{NO}$. Point *N* is the midpoint of $\overline{MP}$.
    4. $\angle MNQ \cong \angle PNO$
    Reasons
    2. definition of midpoint
    3. definition of vertical angles
    4. vertical $\angle$s theorem
    5. SAS postulate
4. 9   5. 70   6. true   7. true   8. false
9. true   10. true
11. < 15 cm and > 3 cm
12. < 6.2 m and > 3.8 m
13. < $3\frac{2}{3}$ yd > 1 yd
14. $\overline{CD}, \overline{DF}, \overline{CF}$
15. 171°
16. 22.5°
17. $a = 3, b = 123, c = 57, d = 5$
18. $a = 45, b = 90, c = 3.5, d = 3.5$
19. 9
20. $\angle G = \angle H = 68°$; $\angle J = \angle I = 112°$
21. If $\overline{AB}$ is congruent to $\overline{DB},$ then $\overline{AB}$ is congruent to $\overline{BC}$.

22.

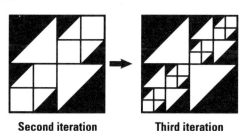

Second iteration   →   Third iteration

ACHIEVEMENT 4B

1. 108
2. 67
3. **Statements**
     3. $\angle ONP = 90°$ and $\angle MNP = 90°$
     4. $m\angle ONP = m\angle MNP$ or $\angle ONP \cong \angle MNP$
     5. $\overline{PN} \cong \overline{PN}$
   Reasons
     1. given
     2. def of perp. lines
     5. reflexive property
     6. ASA postulate
4. 45   5. 3   6. true   7. true   8. false
9. false   10. true
11. < 11 cm and > 5 cm
12. < 7.2 ft and > 4.8 ft
13. $< 3\frac{3}{4}$ yd and $> \frac{3}{4}$ yd
14. $\overline{CD}, \overline{CF}, \overline{DF}$
15. 170°
16. 14.4°
17. $a = 3, b = 63, c = 9, d = 63$
18. $a = 2, b = 2, c = 90, d = 17$
19. 35
20. $\angle K = \angle L = 116°; \angle M = \angle N = 64°$

21. Assume point D is the midpoint of $\overline{AC}$.
22.

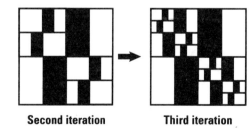

Second iteration   →   Third iteration

ACHIEVEMENT 5A

1. 5.5   2. $3\frac{1}{4}$ 3. 64   4. 3,200   5. 0.435

6. 532   7. $\frac{1}{6}$ 8. $\frac{1}{12}$ 9. $\frac{73}{100}$

10. 23.2 m   11. 23.1 in.   12. 25.12 mm

---

13. 15 m²   14. 285.74 cm²   15. $\frac{1}{4}$ 16. $\frac{91}{100}$

17. Rectangular prism   18. Cone   19. Sphere

Answers may vary for Exercises 20–23; sample answers are given.

20. *ABCDE; FGHIJ*   21. $\overline{CH}$ and $\overline{DI}$

22. *ABCDE* and *EDIJ*   23. $\overline{AE}$ and $\overline{CH}$

24. 550 in.²   25. 132 cm²   26. 18.84 ft²

27. 480 m²   28. 750 in.³   29. 60 cm³

30. 6.28 ft³   31. 720 m³   32. 16.58 mm

33. ± 0.005 mm   34. $\pm \frac{1}{32}$ 35. ± 0.0005 mm

36. ± 0.005 cm   37. Krispy Cereal   38. $\frac{4}{25}$

39. 126 m³
40. Upper: 129.3 mm; Lower: 128.1 mm

ACHIEVEMENT 5B

1. 128   2. $31\frac{1}{2}$ 3. $12\frac{1}{4}$ 4. 9,200   5. 3.56

6. 4,350   7. $\frac{1}{15}$ 8. $\frac{1}{13}$ 9. $\frac{9}{20}$

10. 27.2 m   11. 44.6 cm   12. 37.68 in.

13. 48 m²   14. 263.76 cm²   15. $\frac{1}{5}$ 16. $\frac{21}{25}$

17. Triangular Prism   18. Hexagonal Pyramid
19. Cylinder

Answers may vary for Exercises 20–23; sample answers are given.

20. *ABCDEF; GHIJKL*   21. $\overline{AF}$ and $\overline{CD}$

22. *ABHG* and *BCIH*   23. $\overline{AB}$ and $\overline{DJ}$

24. 1,300 in.²   25. 113.04 cm²   26. 100.48 ft²

27. 1,308 yd²   28. 3,000 in.³   29. 113.04 cm³

30. 75.36 ft³   31. 2,520 yd³   32. 14.71 mm

33. ± 0.005 mm   34. $\pm \frac{1}{16}$ in.   35. ± 0.005 mm

36. ± 0.0005 cm   37. Lo-Saltee's Crackers   38. $\frac{1}{9}$

39. 252 cm²
40. Upper: 146.4 mm; Lower: 144.8 mm

ACHIEVEMENT 6A

1. $\frac{6}{5}$
2. -2
3. $m = 7, b = -2$
4. $y = \frac{1}{2}x - \frac{1}{6}$
5. $\overrightarrow{FG}\ \ m = \frac{-7}{3}, \overrightarrow{HI}\ \ m = \frac{3}{7}$
   perpendicular
6. $l\ \ m = \frac{2}{3}, n\ \ m = 3$
   neither

7. $p\ m = \frac{-7}{2}$, $q\ m = \frac{-14}{4} = \frac{-7}{2}$
   parallel

8. $y = -x + 3$

9. $y = \frac{2}{5}x - 1$

10. $y = \frac{1}{4}x - 1$

11. $y = -\frac{1}{4}x - 3$

12. $(1, -2)$

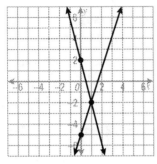

13. The lines are the same. There is an infinite number of solutions.
14. $(6, 4)$
15. There is no solution. The lines are parallel.
16. $(4, -8)$
17. $(8, \frac{9}{2})$
18. $(-14, 30)$
19. 38
20. Tania 18 y, Reginald 3 y
21. 8 L of 70% solution, 24 L of 30% solution
22. 1 mile per hour
23.

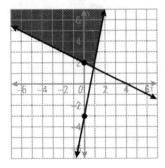

24. 0 at $(0, 0)$

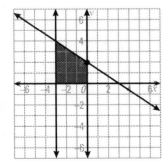

25. 50 tickets

26. a. $\begin{bmatrix} 3 & -5 \\ 1 & 2 \end{bmatrix} \begin{bmatrix} x \\ y \end{bmatrix} = \begin{bmatrix} -10 \\ 4 \end{bmatrix}$

   b. $\det A = \begin{bmatrix} 3 & -5 \\ 1 & 2 \end{bmatrix} = 11$

   c. $(0, 2)$

ACHIEVEMENT 6B

1. 2

2. $\frac{1}{3}$

3. $m = -\frac{2}{7}$, $b = -1$

4. $y = \frac{3}{4}x + \frac{5}{8}$

5. $\overleftrightarrow{FG}\ m = -\frac{1}{3}$, $\overrightarrow{HI}\ m\ -3$
   neither

6. $l\ m = -1$, $n\ m = -1$
   parallel

7. $p\ m = \frac{1}{2}$, $q\ m = 3$
   neither

8. $y = 7x - 21$

9. $y = -x - 1$

10. $y = \frac{1}{3}x + \frac{1}{3}$

11. $y = \frac{2}{3}x - 1$

12. There is no solution. The lines are parallel.

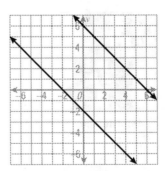

13. $(5, 7)$
14. The lines are the same. There is an infinite number of solutions.
15. $(3, 2)$
16. $(12, 3)$

17. $(-\frac{13}{5}, \frac{5}{2})$
18. (3, –3)
19. 67
20. Toi 15 y, Winnie 23 y
21. 2 lb of black grapes, 6 lb of red grapes
22. 50 miles per hour
23.

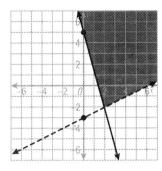

24. –10 at (0, 5)

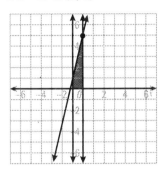

25. 20 tickets

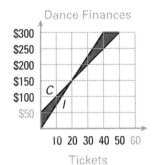

Dance Finances

26. a. $\begin{bmatrix} -7 & 4 \\ 2 & -2 \end{bmatrix}\begin{bmatrix} x \\ y \end{bmatrix} = \begin{bmatrix} 8 \\ -4 \end{bmatrix}$

   b. det $A = \begin{bmatrix} -7 & 4 \\ 2 & -2 \end{bmatrix} = 6$

   c. (0, 2)

ACHIEVEMENT 7A

1. 4   2. 81   3. 46
4. *Explanations may vary. Sample given.*
   Yes, because corresponding angles are congruent

   and corresponding sides are in proportion $(\frac{2}{3})$.

5. 10 cm   6. 10.8 in.   7. 15 m   8. 300 mi
9. 8 in.   10. 4.5 cm   11. SSS   12. AA
13. NO   14. SAS   15. 5   16. 8   17. 9.6
18. 6.8   19. 8   20. 18   21. 3.8   22. 14.4
23. 4
24. *Check students' drawings.*
25. 7.5 lb
26. 9 fl oz
27. *Estimates may vary. Sample given.*
   About 600 pounds
28. *Estimates may vary. Sample given.*
   About 20,000 women
29. 22 ft
30. 30 m

ACHIEVEMENT 7B

1. 15   2. 52   3. 9
4. *Explanations may vary. Sample given.*
   No, because the angles are not congruent. One
   pair of corresponding angles measures 43° and
   45°.

5. 40 cm   6. $3\frac{3}{4}$ in.   7. 22 ft   8. 25 km

9. 12 cm   10. $2\frac{1}{2}$ in.   11. NO   12. SSS
13. SAS   14. AA   15. 16   16. 10.5
17. 12.8   18. 3   19. 1.1   20. 3.8   21. 10
22. 3.3   23. 2
24. *Check students' drawings.*
25. 2.8 gal
26. 12.5 lb
27. *Estimates may vary. Sample given.*
   About 90 computers
28. *Estimates may vary. Sample given.*
   About $450
29. 21 ft
30. 90 mi

ACHIEVEMENT 8A

1.

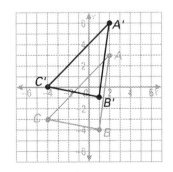

2.

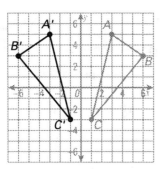

3.

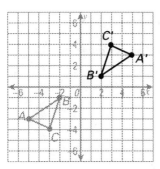

4.

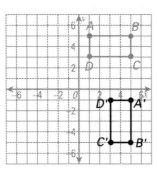

5.

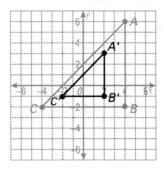

6.

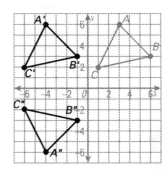

7. (4, 3)

8. (0, 1)

9. Rotation of 180° followed by translation of 6 units up

10. 2×3

11. 8

12. $\begin{bmatrix} 13 & 12 & 15 \\ 7 & 8 & 9 \end{bmatrix}$

13. $\begin{bmatrix} 45 & 10 \\ 5 & 40 \\ 20 & 25 \end{bmatrix}$

14. $\begin{bmatrix} 21 & 16 & 21 \\ 8 & 13 & 16 \end{bmatrix}$

15. $\begin{bmatrix} 74 & 46 & 68 \\ 16 & 44 & 62 \\ 37 & 41 & 59 \end{bmatrix}$

16. $\begin{bmatrix} 149 & 38 & 91 \\ 82 & 17 & 52 \end{bmatrix}$

17. $\begin{bmatrix} 100 & 78 \\ 42 & 77 \end{bmatrix}$

18. $\begin{bmatrix} -1 & -3 & -5 \\ 3 & 2 & 4 \end{bmatrix}$

19. $\begin{bmatrix} 1 & 3 & 5 \\ -3 & -2 & -4 \end{bmatrix}$

20. $4,920

21. $620

ACHIEVEMENT 8B

1.

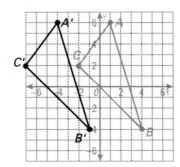

2.

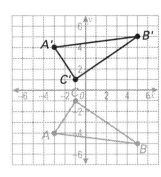

3.

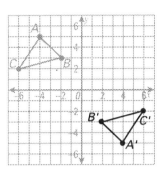

4.

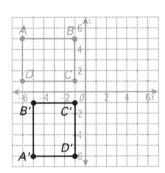

5.

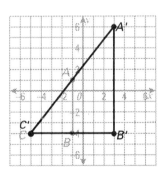

6.

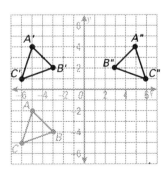

7. (5, 6)
8. (8, 7)
9. Reflections across the *y*-axis followed by 90° clockwise rotation
10. 3 × 2
11. 7

12. $\begin{bmatrix} 10 & 5 & 14 \\ 7 & 15 & 10 \end{bmatrix}$

13. $\begin{bmatrix} 21 & 18 \\ 6 & 9 \\ 15 & 27 \end{bmatrix}$

14. $\begin{bmatrix} 11 & 7 & 22 \\ 10 & 23 & 15 \end{bmatrix}$

15. $\begin{bmatrix} 87 & 63 & 72 \\ 30 & 27 & 27 \\ 81 & 78 & 75 \end{bmatrix}$

16. $\begin{bmatrix} 42 & 78 & 24 \\ 85 & 119 & 63 \end{bmatrix}$

17. $\begin{bmatrix} 60 & 105 & 75 \\ 79 & 114 & 64 \end{bmatrix}$

18. $\begin{bmatrix} 2 & 1 & 3 \\ 1 & 2 & 4 \end{bmatrix}$

19. $\begin{bmatrix} -2 & -1 & -3 \\ -1 & -2 & -4 \end{bmatrix}$

20. $162,750
21. $72,500

ACHIEVEMENT 9A

1. HH, HT, TH, TT
2. $\frac{1}{4}$ or 0.25 or 25%
3. 10 times
4. 25 times
5. $\frac{1}{3}$
6. $\frac{2}{3}$
7. $\frac{2}{13}$
8. $\frac{4}{13}$
9. $\frac{3}{4}$
10. $\frac{3}{50}$
11. $\frac{1}{25}$
12. $\frac{9}{1000}$
13. $\frac{3}{250}$
14. $\frac{2}{15}$
15. $\frac{1}{45}$
16. $\frac{1}{30}$
17. $\frac{1}{60}$
18. Permutation; 720 ways
19. Combination; 21 ways
20. Permutation; 60 ways
21. Combination; 15 ways
22. *Answers may vary. Sample given.*
    About 65 in.
23.

24. 82
25. 50%
26. Above
27. Variance: 2
    Standard deviation: $\sqrt{2}$
28. Variance: 6.8
    Standard deviation: $\sqrt{6.8}$

29. Variance: 5.2
Standard deviation: $\sqrt{5.2}$
30. *Answers will vary.*
31. *Answers will vary. Sample given.*
How many teens were surveyed? Did the sample include teens from 13–19 or was only a small sample age group used? How many products were compared? Why was Acne Zapper preferred?

ACHIEVEMENT 9B

1. HHH, HHT, HTH, THH, TTH, THT, HTT, TTT

2. $\frac{1}{8}$ or 0.125 or 12.5%

3. 7 times   4. 21 times

5. $\frac{1}{3}$ 6. $\frac{2}{3}$ 7. $\frac{4}{13}$ 8. $\frac{12}{13}$ 9. $\frac{2}{13}$

10. $\frac{3}{100}$ 11. $\frac{4}{25}$ 12. $\frac{3}{125}$ 13. $\frac{3}{250}$

14. $\frac{1}{15}$ 15. $\frac{4}{45}$ 16. $\frac{1}{30}$ 17. $\frac{1}{90}$

18. Permutation; 120 ways
19. Combination; 35 ways
20. Combination; 20 ways
21. Permutation; 20 ways
22. *Answers may vary. Sample given.*
About $50
23.

24. 76
25. 50%
26. Above
27. Variance: 6
Standard deviation: $\sqrt{6}$
28. Variance: 4
Standard deviation: $\sqrt{4}$ = 2
29. Variance: 22
Standard deviation: $\sqrt{22}$
30. *Answers will vary.*
31. *Answers will vary. Sample given.*
Does the ad apply only to this store? Is everything on sale? How many items have discounts less than 75%? What is the average discount?

ACHIEVEMENT 10A

1. $7\sqrt{5}$ 2. $3\sqrt{13}$ 3. $4\sqrt{42}$ 4. $\frac{3}{4}$

5. $48\sqrt{10}$ 6. $16\sqrt{6}$ 7. $\frac{\sqrt{26}}{2}$ 8. 7.0 m
9. 13.3 ft 10. 9.4 cm 11. no 12. yes
13. *AC* = 9 m   14. *EF* = $2\sqrt{3}$ in.
CB = $9\sqrt{3}$ m   *DF* = $4\sqrt{3}$ in.
15. *GH* = *GI* = $11\sqrt{2}$ cm
16. *LK* = 8.7 ft
JK = 10.0 ft
17. *MO* = 9.0 mm
MN = 12.7 mm
18. *PQ* = 1.2 yd
QR = 2.3 yd
19. 292° 20. 49° 21. 90° 22. 189° 23. 89°
24. 54° 25. 12 ft 26. 8 cm 27. 7 yd

28. $6\frac{2}{3}$ m 29. 12 in. 30. 5 mm

Check students' constructions for Exercises 31–35; final figure shown.
31.   32.

33. U.S. and state legislators   22°
Judicial and law enforcers   38°
City and county officials   220°
Educators   80°

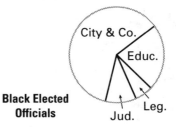

34.   35.

ACHIEVEMENT 10B

1. $15\sqrt{2}$ 2. $8\sqrt{2}$ 3. $8\sqrt{5}$ 4. $\frac{\sqrt{6}}{3}$

5. $16\sqrt{35}$ 6. $18\sqrt{7}$ 7. $\frac{4\sqrt{5}}{5}$ 8. 4.4 m

9. 17.0 yd   10. 9.4 cm   11. yes   12. no

13. $AB = 8$ cm   14. $EF = 6$ in.

   $AC = 8\sqrt{2}$ cm $DF = 6\sqrt{3}$ in.

15. $GH = \frac{16\sqrt{3}}{3}$ cm

   $GI = \frac{32\sqrt{3}}{3}$ cm

16. $LK = 6.9$ in.

   $JK = 8.0$ in.

17. $NO = 9.9$ m

18. $QR = 34.6$ yd

   $PQ = 40$ yd

19. 64°   20. 140°   21. 111°   22. 26°   23. 128°

24. 15°   25. 5 in.   26. 4 cm   27. 13 ft

28. 10 m   29. 18 yd   30. 12 mm

Check students' constructions for Exercises
31–35; final figure shown.

31.   32.

33.

Army	35.9%	129°
Navy	22.4%	81°
Marine Corps	2.0%	7°
Air Force	39.7%	143°

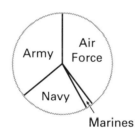

Women Armed Forces Officers

34. 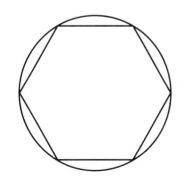   35.

ACHIEVEMENT 11A

1. $6x - 5$ 2. $3n - 1$ 3. $x - 11$ 4. $5y + 8$
5. $-4x^2 + 5xy + 2y^2$ 6. $3a^2 + a - b - 2c$ 7. x^2yz
8. $-10a^3b^2$ 9. $3w^3 - 6wx$ 10. $ab^2 - ac$
11. $-30a^3bc^2$ 12. $56x^3y^2 - 14x^3y^3 + 21x^2y^3$
13. $3(x + 4y)$ 14. $y(5x^2 - 4y)$ 15. $b^2(3ab + 4c)$
16. $2a^2(2 - 3b)$ 17. $4m^2(3m^2 - 2n)$
18. $n^2(8n^2 + 5n - 1)$ 19. $x^2 - 17x + 72$
20. $2b^2 - 3bc - 2c^2$ 21. $12a^2 - 11ab + 2b^2$
22. $(2a + b)(c + 3d)$ 23. $(5w - 2x)(3y - z)$
24. $(4q + 3r)(2s - 5t)$ 25. $(6a - 3b)(2c + d)$
26. $(x + 9)(x + 9)$ or $(x + 9)^2$
27. $(y - 9)(y - 9)$ or $(y - 9)^2$ 28. $(3a + 4)(3a - 4)$
29. $(2y + 7)(2y + 7)$ or $(2y + 7)^2$ 30. $(x + 10)(x - 1)$
31. $(b + 6)(b - 1)$ 32. $(y - 10)(y + 3)$
33. $(a - 6)(a - 2)$ 34. $5(3x + 2)(x - 1)$
35. $(2a + 3)(a + 7)$ 36. $3(c - 1)(2c - 5)$
37. $(7x - 3)(3x + 1)$
38. 1, $2s^2t$; 2, s^2t; 2s, st; s, st; 2t, s^2; t, $2s^2$
39. $4c$ 40. $7r^2s$

ACHIEVEMENT 11B

1. $3x + 1$ 2. $4n - 9$ 3. $-2x + 6$ 4. $11y - 4$
5. $6x^2 + 14xy + 6y^2$ 6. $2a^2 - 4a + b + 2c$ 7. a^3bc
8. $-28x^3y^3$ 9. $7xy^2 - 28xz$ 10. $xy^2 - xz$
11. $48a^3bc$ 12. $15a^4b^3 - 9a^4b^4 + 12a^3b^4$
13. $2(m + 4n)$ 14. $ab(7a - 3b)$ 15. $x(2y^3 + 5xy)$
16. $3m^2(1 + 2n)$ 17. $5a^3(2a - b^2)$
18. $x^3(7x^2 - 2x + 1)$ 19. $x^2 - 10x + 21$
20. $3r^2 - 8rs - 3s^2$ 21. $10x^2 - 9xy + 2y^2$
22. $(6w - 2x)(y - z)$ 23. $(15a - 3b)(c + 2d)$
24. $(5q + 2r)(s + 2t)$ 25. $(3a - 6b)(c + 4d)$
26. $(x + 2)(x + 2)$ or $(x + 2)^2$
27. $(y - 5)(y - 5)$ or $(y - 5)^2$ 28. $(2a - 5)(2a + 5)$
29. $(3y + 5)(3y + 5)$ or $(3y + 5)^2$ 30. $(x + 3)(x + 2)$
31. $(b - 3)(b - 1)$ 32. $(y + 8)(y - 2)$
33. $(a + 7)(a + 1)$ 34. $2(x + 3)(x + 9)$
35. $(2a + 5)(a - 5)$ 36. $(7c - 1)(c + 3)$
37. $(8x - 3)(2x - 5)$
38. 1, $3xy^2$; 3, xy^2; 3x, y^2; 3xy, y; 3y, xy; $3y^2$, x
39. $5ab^2$ 40. $8ab^2$

ACHIEVEMENT 12A

1. $(0, 1)$ 2. $(0, 4)$

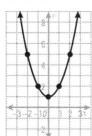

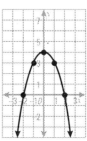

3. (0, –1)

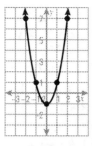

4. Vertex: (1, 2)
Line of symmetry: $x = 1$

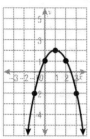

5. Vertex: $(-\frac{1}{2}, -2\frac{1}{4})$
Line of symmetry: $x = -\frac{1}{2}$

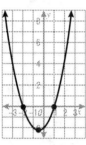

6. Vertex: $(-1\frac{1}{2}, -\frac{1}{4})$
Line of symmetry: $x = -1\frac{1}{2}$

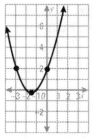

7. No   8. Yes   9. Yes   10. No solution
11. $x = 3, x = 1$ 12. $x = -7, x = 4$
13. $x = 5, x = 2$ 14. $x^2 - 4x + 4$ 15. $x^2 + 8x + 16$
16. $x = -12, x = 2$ 17. $x = 5, x = 1$
18. $x = 1, x = -9$ 19. $x = 3, x = -1$
20. $x = -2, x = -1$ 21. $x = 3, x = 1$
22. $x = \frac{-1 \pm \sqrt{7}}{2}$ 23. $x = 1 \pm \sqrt{5}$

24. $\sqrt{10} \approx 3.2$ units   25. $\sqrt{41} \approx 6.4$ units
26. $\sqrt{100} = 10$ units   27. $\sqrt{8} \approx 2.8$ units
28. $(-\frac{1}{2}, 1)$ 29. $(1\frac{1}{2}, 4)$ 30. 121 ft

ACHIEVEMENT 12B

1. (0, 3)

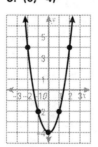

2. (0, 6)

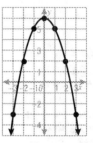

3. (0, –4)

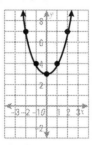

4. Vertex: (1, –2)
Line of symmetry: $x = 1$

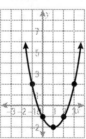

5. Vertex: $(-1\frac{1}{2}, -4\frac{1}{4})$
Line of symmetry: $x = -1\frac{1}{2}$

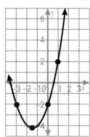

6. Vertex: $(1\frac{1}{2}, 4\frac{1}{4})$

Line of symmetry: $x = 1\frac{1}{2}$

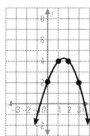

7. Yes   8. No   9. Yes   10. $x = 2$, $x = -1$
11. No solution   12. $x = -4$, $x = 3$
13. $x = -3$, $x = -1$ 14. $x^2 + 2x + 1$
15. $x^2 + 4x + 4$ 16. $x = 7$, $x = 1$
17. $x = 1$, $x = 11$ 18. $x = 13$, $x = 1$
19. $x = -3$, $x = 1$ 20. $x = -8$, $x = 2$ 21. $x = 1$
22. $x = -2$, $x = 1\frac{1}{2}$ 23. $x = 2 \pm \sqrt{5}$
24. $\sqrt{13} \approx 3.6$ 25. $\sqrt{26} \approx 5.1$ 26. $\sqrt{32} \approx 5.7$
27. $\sqrt{1} = 1$ 28. $(3, -2)$ 29. $(\frac{1}{2}, -1)$
30. 225 ft

ACHIEVEMENT 13A

1. $(x - 2)^2 + (y - 5)^2 = 16$
2. $(x + 3)^2 + (y - 4)^2 = 49$
3. $x^2 + y^2 = 25$
4. $r = 11$; center $(0, 0)$
5. $r = 4$; center $(4, -2)$
6. $r = \sqrt{13}$; center $(-3, -2)$
7. F $(0, 6)$; D $(y = -6)$
8. F $(0, -3)$; D $(y = 3)$
9. F $(0, 2)$; D $(y = -2)$
10. $x^2 = -24y$ 11. $x^2 = 32y$ 12. $x^2 = -y$
13. Circle   14. 2 Triangles   15. Parabola
16. $5x^2 + 9y^2 = 45$ 17. $25x^2 - 9y^2 = 225$
18.

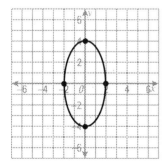

19.

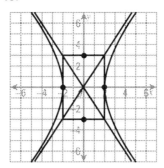

20. $y = 0.5x$ 21. $y = 0.875x$
22. $y = \frac{7.8}{x}$ 23. $y = \frac{46}{x}$
24.

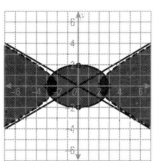

25.

26. 64 g   27. 6 h   28. 5%

ACHIEVEMENT 13B

1. $(x + 5)^2 + (y + 2)^2 = 81$
2. $x^2 + y^2 = 9$
3. $(x + 2)^2 + (y - 3)^2 = 64$
4. $r = 13$; center $(0, 0)$
5. $r = 8$; center $(7, -3)$
6. $r = \sqrt{19}$; center $(-9, -5)$
7. F $(0, 8)$; D $(y = -8)$
8. F $(0, \frac{5}{2})$; D $(y = -\frac{5}{2})$
9. F $(0, 3)$; D $(y = -3)$
10. $x^2 = 8y$ 11. $x^2 = -28y$ 12. $x^2 = -\frac{1}{2}y$
13. Ellipse   14. Circle   15. 2 Triangles
16. $9x^2 + 25y^2 = 225$ 17. $16x^2 - 4y^2 = 64$

18.

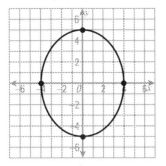

19.

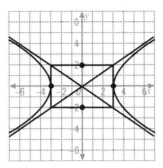

20. y = 0.5

21. y = 0.625

22. $y = \frac{6.3}{x}$

23. $y = \frac{40}{x}$

24.

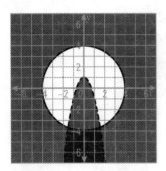

25.

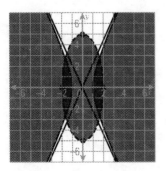

26. 40 g   **27.** 5 h   **28.** 7%

ACHIEVEMENT 14A

1. $\frac{7}{25}$ **2.** $\frac{7}{25}$ **3.** $\frac{24}{25}$ **4.** $\frac{7}{24}$ **5.** $\frac{24}{25}$

6. $\frac{24}{7}$

7. DF: 11.4 cm
m∠D: 38°
EF: 9.0 m

8. m∠H: 74°
GI: 17.3 ft
m∠I: 16°

9. JL: 15.0 cm
m∠L: 37°
m∠J: 53°

10. MO: 22.7 yd
m∠M: 18°
MN: 21.6 yd

11. $-\frac{\sqrt{2}}{2}$

12. $\frac{1}{2}$

13. $\frac{\sqrt{2}}{2}$

14. $\frac{\sqrt{3}}{2}$

15. $\frac{\sqrt{3}}{2}$

16. $-\frac{\sqrt{3}}{2}$

17.

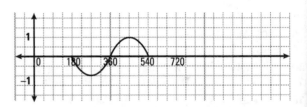

18.

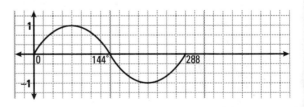

19. 288°
20. Period: 120°
    Amplitude: 5
    Position: Up 9 units
21. Period: 720°
    Amplitude: 2
    Position: Down 4 units
22. Period: 45°
    Amplitude: 1.5
    Position: Down 2 units
23. Period: 180°
    Amplitude: 3
    Position: Up 1 unit
24. 126.9 ft   25. 19.6 ft   26. 503.5 ft   27. 17°

ACHIEVEMENT 14B

1. $\frac{60}{61}$ 2. $\frac{11}{61}$ 3. $\frac{11}{61}$ 4. $\frac{11}{60}$ 5. $\frac{60}{61}$

6. $\frac{60}{11}$

7. *DF*: 16.6 m
   $m\angle E$: 67°
   $m\angle F$: 23°
8. $m\angle H$: 75°
   GI: 6.5 ft
   HI: 24.1 ft
9. $m\angle J$: 37°
   $m\angle L$: 53°
   JK: 16 mm
10. *MN*: 8 yd
    NO: 3.9 yd
    $m\angle N$: 61°

11. $\frac{1}{2}$

12. $\frac{\sqrt{3}}{2}$

13. $-\frac{\sqrt{2}}{2}$

14. $-\frac{\sqrt{2}}{2}$

15. $-\frac{1}{2}$

16. $-\frac{\sqrt{3}}{2}$

17.

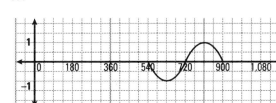

18.

19. 2
20. Period: 180°
    Amplitude: 4
    Position: Down 1 unit
21. Period: 240°
    Amplitude: 5
    Position: Up 2 units
22. Period: 72°
    Amplitude: 6
    Position: Down 7 units
23. Period: 90°
    Amplitude: 3
    Position: Up 4 units
24. 78.1 ft   25. 18.8 ft   26. 14°   27. 354.9 ft

ACHIEVEMENT FINAL A

1. 72   2. $\frac{1}{16}$ 3. –216   4. 2

5. $\{a\}, \{b\}, \{a, b\}, \varnothing$ 6. 14   7. 13   8. –4

9. 7   10. $n = -7$ 11. $b = \frac{4}{9}$ 12. $m \le -6$

13. $d > 24$ 14. 90°   15. 45°   16. 135°
17. 45°
18. If two lines are not parallel, then they intersect.
    Statement: T; Converse: F

19. $\overline{XY}, \overline{YZ}, \overline{XZ}$ 20. True   21. True
22. 16 cm   23. 15:7   24. 3:29

25. $\frac{9}{100}$, 0.09, or 9%   26. 608 ft^2 27. 768 ft^3
28. 0   29. –4   30. $y = -2x - 2$

31. $x = 2\frac{1}{4}$; $y = 3$ 32. $x = 3$; $y = \frac{1}{6}$
33. $x = 5$; $y = 2$ 34. 89   35. SSS
36. NO   37. AA   38. 4.3   39. 7.5
40. 13.5   41. 14 fl oz
42.

43.

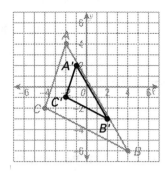

44. $\begin{bmatrix} 13 & 10 & 14 \\ 5 & 11 & 13 \end{bmatrix}$ **45.** $\begin{bmatrix} 36 & 20 & 24 \\ 8 & 36 & 32 \end{bmatrix}$

46. $\begin{bmatrix} 63 & 98 & 88 \\ 33 & 55 & 53 \end{bmatrix}$

47. $\frac{1}{4}$, 0.25, or 25%   **48.** $\frac{4}{13}$ **49.** 120 ways

50. 56 ways   **51.** 37   **52.** 8 cm

53. *CB*: 17.3 ft   **54.** *DF*: 8 m
  AB: 20 ft   *DE*: 11.3 m

55. *GH*: 12.5 yd
  GI: 21.7 yd

56. 49°   **57.** 2 in.   **58.** 77°   **59.** $2x + 5$

60. $2x^2 + 14x - 36$ **61.** $3a$ **62.** $(x + 3)(x - 1)$

63. $(3a + 1)(2a - 6)$ **64.** $4b$

65. $(0, -3)$ **66.** Vertex: $(-2, -2)$
                 Axis: $x = -2$

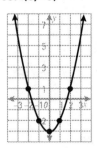   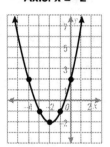

67. $x = 2; x = -1\frac{1}{3}$

68. $x = 3 \pm 2\sqrt{3}$ **69.** $x^2 = -16y$

70. $16x^2 + 25y^2 = 400$ **71.** $y = 91.2$ **72.** $y = 16.8$

73. 60°   **74.** 8.7 cm   **75.** 30°   **76.** 25 ft

ACHIEVEMENT FINAL B

1. 72   **2.** $\frac{1}{4}$ **3.** 36   **4.** 2

5. $\{x\}, \{y\}, \{x, y\}, \varnothing$ **6.** 15   **7.** 6   **8.** –1   **9.** 31

10. $n = 4$ **11.** $x = -2\frac{1}{4}$ **12.** $p < 2$

13. $k \geq 32$ **14.** 180°   **15.** 90°   **16.** 132°

17. 132°

18. If two lines are coplanar, then they intersect.
  Statement: T; Converse: F

19. $\overline{XY}, \overline{XZ}, \overline{YZ}$ **20.** False   **21.** True

22. 17 cm   **23.** 9:4   **24.** 5:82

25. $\frac{1}{5}$, 0.2, or 20%   **26.** 492 ft^2 **27.** 504 ft^3

28. $-\frac{1}{2}$ **29.** 6   **30.** $y = 3x$ **31.** $x = 7; y = -2$

32. $x = 1; y = -2$ **33.** $x = -2; y = -2\frac{1}{2}$ **34.** 42

35. SAS   **36.** NO   **37.** SSS   **38.** 6.7   **39.** 15

40. 8.3   **41.** $5\frac{1}{4}$ fl oz

42.

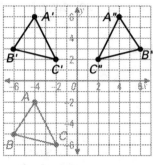
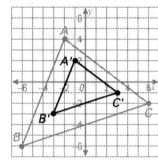

43.

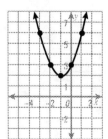

44. $\begin{bmatrix} 13 & 10 & 14 \\ 5 & 11 & 13 \end{bmatrix}$ **45.** $\begin{bmatrix} 12 & 15 & 24 \\ 9 & 6 & 15 \end{bmatrix}$ **46.** $\begin{bmatrix} 74 & 87 & 101 \\ 85 & 120 & 94 \end{bmatrix}$

47. $\frac{3}{8}$, 0.375, or 37.5%   **48.** $\frac{4}{13}$ **49.** 720 ways

50. 56 ways   **51.** 70   **52.** 4 cm

53. *AC*: 34.6 m   **54.** *AC*: 17.0 m
  BC: 40 m   *AB*: 12 m

55. *AB*: 15 ft
  BC: 26.0 ft

56. 6 m   **57.** 72°   **58.** 34°   **59.** $x + 5$

60. $2x^2 - 10x - 28$ **61.** $4ab$ **62.** $(x + 6)(x - 2)$

63. $(3a + 4)(2a - 1)$ **64.** $2a$

65. $(0, -1)$ **66.** Vertex: $(-1, 2)$
                 Axis: $x = -1$

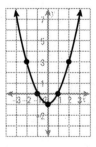

67. $x = -2; x = \frac{2}{3}$

68. $x = \frac{1 \pm \sqrt{33}}{4}$ **69.** $x^2 = 12y$

70. $12x^2 + 4y^2 = 48$ **71.** $y = 70$ **72.** $y = 16$

73. 48°   **74.** 42°

75. 8.9 m   **76.** 20 ft

SOLUTIONS FOR CHAPTER EVALUATIONS

Chapter 1

Answers wlil vary. Possible answers:
Numbers between 0 and 1:

$$\{\tfrac{1}{4},\ 0.25,\ 0.00932,\ 1.7 \times 105\}$$

Numbers less than 0:

$$\{-13.9,\ -1|-5|\}$$

Numbers greater than 1:

$$\{|12|,\ 7,\ \sqrt{5},\ 740{,}0000,\ 0.3 \times 10^9\}$$

Chapter 2

Answers will vary. Possible answers:

Speed on a Center Street

Speed mi/h	Number of Cars
0–9	15
10–19	30
20–29	25
30–39	45
40–49	20

Chapter 3

Answers will vary. Some postulates will change. For instance, on a globe, the shortest distance between two points is an arc of a great circle containing those two points.

Chapter 4

$\triangle ADB$ and $\triangle ADC$ are right triangles.
$\triangle ADB$ and $\triangle ADC$ are congruent.
Proof:

AD is perpendicular bisector of BC—given
$\angle ADB \cong \angle ADC$—they are both right angles
$\overline{AD} \cong \overline{AD}$—reflexive property
$\overline{BD} \cong \overline{DC}$—definition of bisector
$\triangle ADB \cong \triangle ABC$—ASA Postulate

Chapter 5

Answers will vary. Check students' work to be sure each question is answered. Students should decide whether the containers will be shipped already assembled (such as a large cup or tub) or folded (such as a foldable box).

Chapter 6

Answers will vary. Possible answers:
$x = -5$: Slope undefined, no y-intercept
$y = 4$: slope = 0, y-intercept = 4
$y = 4x + 24$: Slope = 4, y-intercept = 24

$2x + 3y = 2$: Slope = $-\tfrac{2}{3}$, y-intercept = $\tfrac{2}{3}$

Chapter 7

Answers will vary.
For the scale drawing, measurements such as total height, length of legs, width of head, etc. will be needed. For a scale model, measurements such as distance around waist and head will be needed.

Chapter 8

Answers will vary. For students who are intimidated by the idea of doing art work, encourage them to keep their logos simple.

Chapter 9

Green Cremlins have the best batting average. Their median is the highest.

Chapter 10

Answers will vary. Possible answer:

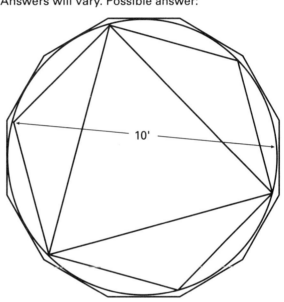

Chapter 11

Answers will vary. Possible answer:

x	x	1	1	1
x	x	1	1	1
x	x	1	1	1
x^2	x^2	x	x	x
x^2	x^2	x	x	x

$2x + 3$ (vertical)

$2x + 3$ (horizontal)

$(2x + 3)^2 = 4x^2 + 12x + 9$
There are 3 terms so it is a trinomial.
It is equal to $(2x + 3)^2$ so it is a perfect square.
The binomial factors are $2x + 3$ and $2x + 3$.

Chapter 12

Yes. Explanations may vary.

Chapter 13

Answers will vary. Possible equations:

If initials are AF:
  A. Direct Variation: F = 3A
  B. Direct Square Variation: F = 2A^2
  C. Inverse Variation: F = 4/A
  D. Inverse Square Variation: F = 6/A^2
Check students' graphs.

Chapter 14

Answers will vary. Possible answer:

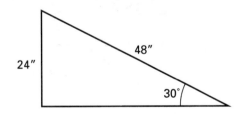

24″, 48″, 30°

Ramp will be 48″ (4 ft) long and the angle of incline will be 30°.

Note: Sin 30° = $\frac{24}{48}$ = $\frac{1}{2}$

ANSWERS FOR CUMULATIVE TEST

Chapter 1

1. D	2. A	3. D	4. C
5. B	6. B	7. A	8. C
9. C	10. D	11. B	12. D
13. A	14. A	15. C	16. B
17. A			

Chapter 2

1. D	2. A	3. A	4. D
5. C	6. B	7. B	8. C
9. D	10. A	11. B	12. A
13. B	14. C	15. D	16. C

Chapter 3

1. B	2. C	3. D	4. D
5. A	6. C	7. A	8. D
9. C	10. B	11. B	12. A
13. B	14. A	15. C	

Chapter 4

1. D	2. D	3. A	4. C
5. A	6. B	7. C	8. D
9. A	10. D	11. B	12. A
13. B	14. C	15. B	

Chapter 5

1. A	2. B	3. A	4. D
5. B	6. C	7. C	8. A
9. A	10. D	11. B	12. C
13. C	14. D	15. D	

Chapter 6

1. C	2. A	3. B	4. C
5. D	6. D	7. A	8. C
9. B	10. D	11. A	12. C
13. B	14. A		

Chapter 7

1. D	2. A	3. D	4. C
5. B	6. C	7. A	8. D
9. C	10. B	11. B	12. C
13. A	14. A	15. B	

Chapter 8

1. D	2. C	3. C	4. A
5. B	6. B	7. A	8. C
9. D	10. A	11. B	12. C
13. B	14. A		

Chapter 9

1. A	2. D	3. D	4. B
5. C	6. B	7. C	8. A
9. B	10. C	11. A	12. C
13. B	14. B	15. D	

Chapter 10

1. C	**2.** A	**3.** D	**4.** D
5. B	**6.** A	**7.** A	**8.** B
9. D	**10.** A	**11.** C	**12.** C
13. B			

Chapter 11

1. D	**2.** C	**3.** A	**4.** A
5. C	**6.** B	**7.** D	**8.** B
9. A	**10.** C	**11.** D	**12.** B
13. A	**14.** C		

Chapter 12

1. B	**2.** C	**3.** A	**4.** A
5. D	**6.** B	**7.** A	**8.** C
9. D	**10.** B	**11.** C	**12.** D
13. A	**14.** C	**15.** B	

Chapter 13

1. C	**2.** C	**3.** A	**4.** D
5. B	**6.** C	**7.** A	**8.** A
9. D	**10.** B	**11.** B	**12.** C
13. A	**14.** D	**15.** B	

Chapter 14

1. B	**2.** A	**3.** C	**4.** A
5. B	**6.** B	**7.** D	**8.** A
9. B	**10.** C	**11.** A	**12.** D
13. B	**14.** A	**15.** A	**16.** C
17. A	**18.** D	**19.** B	**20.** B
21. C	**22.** A	**23.** D	**24.** B
25. C	**26.** B	**27.** D	**28.** A
29. A	**30.** D		

Teacher's Notes

Teacher's Notes

Teacher's Notes